LOVINGLY LIBERATED

A Christian woman's response
to the liberation movement

LOVINGLY
LIBERATED

Sandie Chandler

Fleming H. Revell Company
Old Tappan, New Jersey

Library of Congress Cataloging in Publication Data

Chandler, Sandie.
   Lovingly liberated.
   /22p. ; 21 cm.
   1. Feminism--United States. 2. Women--Religious life. I. Title.
HQ1426.C457   261.8'34'12   75–20141
ISBN 0–8007–0750–8

TO my daughters, Holly and Heather,
and to all girls and women
who desire to be lovingly liberated

Acknowledgments

The author wishes to express appreciation to her husband who edited the manuscript and became her chief critic, to the many individuals who filled out questionnaires, and to Fleming H. Revell Company for permission to use portions of *Time Out, Ladies.*

Contents

Nevertheless, in the Lord woman is not independent of man nor man of woman; for as woman was made from man, so man is now born of woman. And all things are from God.

1 Corinthians 11:11,12 RSV

Introduction

I am going through one of the most terrifying periods of my life. For seventeen years I have felt that I was a liberated woman and now I'm discovering it has been a big farce!

To those who have known me, this will come as shock. Others—like you—will immediately identify with me because you, too, have been through or are going through an inner struggle. If not, prepare yourself—it could happen at any time.

After I was married I moved three thousand miles from my family, friends, and familiar surroundings. I developed a new life-style. I explored a large city for the first time in my life. I shopped without the advice of my mother. I joined my husband in making major professional decisions and in deciding where to live. After my husband completed graduate school, we left the East and returned to the West Coast where I met with grave illness, pursued my bachelor's degree in education, and took on church and community responsibilities. I gained new insights about the world and about myself. I saw myself as unique—a woman God created for a purpose. Five years after our wedding we were blessed with a daughter, Heather; two years later we had another daughter, Holly; six years after that a son, Timothy.

By teaching before our children were born, I experienced a certain professionalism. After the birth of our daughters,

I substituted and did private tutoring and Title I Remedial Reading on a part-time basis.

Motherhood brought me great fulfillment. I realized I had been given the awesome responsibility of raising God's children. With their birth, I experienced a deeper awareness of God's grace, His power to strengthen physically as well as spiritually and emotionally. It was a blessing to be chosen by Him to raise His children. I found nothing oppressive about motherhood then. I still don't. Yes, there were times when I had to get out of the house for a little while. What mother doesn't feel that way? With the exception of leading Bible studies, directing choirs, and being a member of such organizations as the American Association of University Women, the Parent-Teacher Association, and the Capitol Speakers Club of Washington, D.C.—as well as doing some counseling—my major role has been wife and mother. I have been involved in enough activities to keep aware of what's going on in the world, yet not so many that I built a wall of separation between me and my family.

Many people have said to me, "Gosh, Sandie, you've really got it all together. You're the most liberated woman I know."

What you will learn about me is that I am typical of many women. Because of my personal encounter with liberation I feel qualified to write about the lessons I have learned and to challenge you to adopt necessary changes in your life.

The Holy Spirit taught me the greatest lessons of a lifetime as I sincerely sought to become more liberated in Christ's love. Every possible emotion has been dealt with—and none has been all good. I have thrown this manuscript on the floor and packed reference books away. Once, over a twenty-four-hour period, I came to realize that maybe I wasn't liberated at all. I found myself saying, "Every time I sit down and try to think, let alone write, one of my children is asking me a question. Or two of them are fighting and they need some guidance. For some reason they have never behaved so badly before! What is God trying to say to me through all this?"

The feelings of frustration I have had have been almost unbearable. I think about my oldest child, Heather, who is entering those vital preadolescent years. Emotional years. Years during which—if I turn her off—I will break future communication. She needs a confidante. I have been that person—am I willing to relinquish such an honor? With the desire I have to pursue this book and several others, as well as to continue to fulfill speaking engagements, there is a good chance I could turn her off—maybe for the next six years, maybe for a lifetime.

As I think about my second child, Holly, I see some emotional needs because of competition with her sister. She has just begun orthodontic treatment. Last week she had four teeth extracted. A few days ago she looked in the mirror and tried to assess how she will look when the work is completed. She wonders if she will ever do as well academically as her sister. I know her talent potential and I know God has a beautiful plan for her life. I do not know how He will use her but it will be in a dynamic way—providing she is given the depth of love that her sensitive soul needs.

And there is Timothy. He yearns to go to school. His mind is extremely active and alert. It is impossible for him to understand why some of his friends are going to kindergarten and he claims, "They don't even know the colors or letters or shapes and they can't even count to one hundred." Precocious, yes—but he also has many talents still unrecognized not only by himself but also by us. One day recently he said, "Let the girls sit in the back of the camper and I'll sit in the pickup with you. We can have a special time together." When needs such as these are so openly expressed, I must listen. I have taught all our children to verbalize—now I must listen to their verbalization.

I often ask, "Oh, God, what are You trying to say to me? Am I supposed to give up the drive, the feeling I have inside that You can use me in writing and speaking?" And after reflecting on my life and adding up the cost, I painfully, with a throbbing heart and a tear-drenched face answer, "Yes, I will give it up. I will give it up because I am only one life, and my children represent three times myself. More important, I have a husband—so my influence is felt on four lives."

After exploding one night at the height of my struggle for self-identity, I realized that when I was so upset Russ didn't know what to say or how to say it. Part of the time he did a terrible job. He made me antagonistic toward him. But oh, he loves me. And I love him. And if I can't support him—if I can't give him emotional and spiritual love as well as intellectual stimulation—then how can he function as the breadwinner in our family?

So you see, dear God, there are really four lives involved and I am just one—but a very important one! My liberation is to be based on the liberation I allow my loved ones because of Your great love that liberated me. I have come to this realization intellectually. I cannot yet handle it emotionally. So I will let the tears flow, and if my stomach gets all tied up I will praise You for knowing my real needs.

Perhaps I have experienced the great frustration that so many women know, and have no answer for, because God wants to use me in some way. My Lord loves me and He has a great plan for my life, and I know beyond a shadow

16

of a doubt that He will, in His time, use me. But now I must remember to hold close to my heart Christ's promise:

> If you love me, obey me; and I will ask the Father and he will give you another Comforter, and he will never leave you. . . . I will not abandon you or leave you as orphans in the storm—I will come to you.
>
> John 14:15,18

Yes, it's the Comforter I need now for I am so human. I long to succeed professionally, to get into the world and be used by God. But if I move forth with this drive and forsake my family, I shall deprive the world of four times what He could do in my life. I believe I see what liberation is experientially: It is to be free. It is to make those you love free, and in so doing, to come to know your own liberation.

LOVINGLY LIBERATED

1
Learning About Liberation

Feminine oppression is talked about in church and community groups. It is hassled between husband and wife, parents and children.

Not long ago, four San Francisco policewomen were taken off duty because they supposedly lacked the strength to handle resisters. At the same time, women were making headlines on Wall Street. The financial world is becoming a new area of command for the "gentle sex."

The California State Division of Forestry has started to hire women in outdoor jobs. Officials are discovering that women have good rapport with the public.

The House of Representatives, the last federal male stronghold, recently acquired a female page. The Senate and the Supreme Court have had them for years.

Coeds are rowing at Radcliff College. They find the routine grueling but the gregarious girls are grooving on the experience.

Every magazine and newspaper in the country has featured stories on Women's Liberation. In some areas, because of the attention that is being given to Women's Liberation, the men are now feeling oppressed.

Women are refusing to talk about history. Instead, it is "herstory." Carl Samra, dismayed by Betty Friedan's book *The Feminine Mystique,* wrote *The Feminine Mistake.*

Where the Liberation Movement will end no one knows. One thing is sure: We are all affected through legislation, life-styles, and the process of learning who we are, why we're here, and where we're going.

I want to focus on the need for liberation for each of us —the need to know ourselves, the need to believe in ourselves.

Too often a person views the role of woman in relation to his or her own background. If an individual has been raised to believe a woman's place is in the home, then the role of a woman active in society or a profession is seen as wrong. On the other hand, a person may grow up with a working mother and believe that anything short of professional status is degrading.

Our changing society needs to remain objective about the roles played by both men and women. From the most primitive societies to the most sophisticated, women have had to live in relation to their parents, husbands, neighbors, and selves. As daughters, we have been expected to adhere to certain standards, and to perform particular jobs. As wives, our duties may have been in mothering and/or sexual relationships. As an individual responsible only to self, a woman must nevertheless make decisions which relate to others.

During the past ten years the Liberation Movement has grown more rapidly in understanding and power than in the previous one hundred years. Still, many avoid everything associated with the word "liberation" because it is distasteful. It suggests lesbianism, demonstrations, and bra burning. For some, it is just that. But for others it is a contemporary handle on which to work through an identity crisis.

Psychologically, we think of children and adolescents as having identity crises. Actually, more women today than ever before are faced with the fears and frustrations of being a woman. These feelings are unnecessary, but because they are present in so many lives they must be dealt with.

I have known a number of women, including myself, who lead happy, wholesome, fulfilled lives. But there is a time—maybe only once in a lifetime, maybe more—when one feels the need to take stock. The best way to recognize this is to ask, "Who am I? What do I want to do with my life five, ten, twenty years from now? What are my values? What should I keep as part of my life and what should be done away with?" This is the beginning of an identity crisis. It is nothing to be feared if it is dealt with rationally and within a reasonable amount of time. Professional counseling may be in order. But most likely, if you are able to recognize yourself through what you have just read, then together we can explore the lessons of liberation.

Don't forget that the person who is *going through* this time of growth is no less a person than the one who merely *thinks* of doing something with her life. Maybe going through it makes us just a bit more intense. Whatever it is, there is nothing to be ashamed of. It's real! Praise the Lord, we are able to deal with it, providing we are willing to learn.

Learning about our unique identity in today's world is apt to be time-consuming. It can be painful as well as filled with new self-revelations.

One day as I was thinking about the best way for me to learn about the liberated life, I saw a butterfly rest upon a large Shasta daisy. The grace the butterfly displayed as it rested on that flower made me envious. It had no cares but to acquire the flower's nectar and to enjoy resting on the bright yellow center.

I long for times like that. You undoubtedly do, too. But as I watched that butterfly I realized that its beauty had developed through various biological changes. As a caterpillar it crawled from twig to leaf and along the dirt searching for particles of food to help it grow. As infants we are brought into a world void of meaning. Our bodies are nourished and because God created us as His ultimate beings, we were able to feel love, hate, tenderness, irritability, joy, and rejection, among other essential emotions. The way we relate to life now is dependent upon those early years.

But the poor little caterpillar—he can only crawl. At the proper biological time, he finds a good limb and starts to spin a cocoon. His life becomes one of hibernation. So our childhood, like the cocoon stage, is wrapped up in the family unit. Or so it could have been. How we are able to accept our maleness or femaleness goes back to those years when we were children.

Did we play with brothers and sisters, boys and girls? Did we paint, dig in the dirt, collect snakes, play dolls, and bake cookies, regardless of sex? This is part of what liberation is all about. This is the good part of liberation—being able to be *you*—not a rebellious woman fighting society and making unjust accusations toward men.

As parents and grandparents, we find that being liberated provides the ability not only to seek our own identities but also to expand and enrich the lives of the children who come in contact with us. We can reach out with love and understanding and draw them into a warm atmosphere where they not only *feel* but *know* they are unique.

So the cocoon and our childhood years are set aside for further development. When the cocoon reaches a certain stage, its outer layer starts to change. So do we start to change at adolescence. That is the time just before we emerge into total responsibility for ourselves—a time when the warm security of a silk skin will not be protecting us from the world, a time when we will have the opportunity to move freely.

If in the course of development the pupa drops or is mutilated, its life—the beauty we see in its wings or the way it flies—will be noticeably altered. Adolescence is the same way. We recognize the tremendous needs youth have today: not just physical care, but moral support—the touch of a hand on a shoulder to say, "I know it's difficult but I'm proud of you and I know you can do it." These years will be used by God to allow us as parents to reinforce God's teachings and His plan for liberation—the freedom to move into a world of which none of us is sure.

Then comes emergence—not instantly, but gradually. The insect that was once a caterpillar begins to emerge into the world of flowers and trees. It now has the capacity to fly to heights unknown to us. The butterfly shows mankind its grace and beauty as well as its liberation.

So do we. Once we emerge into the world of decisions and daydreams, we find we have the freedom to choose what we want. But even with our freedom, we allow our intellect and emotional structure to burden us—keeping us oppressed.

Only when we learn the lessons for liberation can we fly to the heights God's plan intended for our lives.

2

The Self-on-the-Shelf Syndrome

Too frequently our thoughts and actions are so cloistered in the thou-shalt and the thou-shalt-nots of Christianity that we forget our emotions are human. I have fallen victim to the feminists' cry of "UNFAIR." Until recently I believed I was liberated. I have not only chosen when to give birth, care for, and train my children but I have also been able to supervise a house, yard, and car.

"Of course I'm liberated, what more freedom could I want?" has been my oft-repeated cry. My husband has been a large part of every aspect of my life, but there is very little that I couldn't do if required. Being a team has made the difference between tasks being routine drudgery or creative experience.

I am now approximately halfway through my life, and just recently I realized that there may be something more. Maybe I have missed out on something, or maybe I shouldn't have gotten married when I did. Whatever it is, I need to reevaluate what has gone on in the years since our partnership began. The joys I have shared with my husband require not only that I remember instances but also that I reflect on the meaning they have given to our relationship and to my life.

During this reevaluation, I should have my attention focused on the way we place ourselves on a shelf without giving thought to the potential dynamism we contain within.

A majority of women get hung up in one or more of three areas. They worry because they are nothing more than "swingless singles," have problems being professional persons, or moan about motherhood.

It's not unusual to hear a swingless single exclaim, "It's no use! I'll never get married. I've nothing to offer." Poor girl. She's really got the blahs. Where is her *self* concept? Quite frankly, maybe she never had one! And if she did, something tore it down.

If this is you, think right now about why you are a swingless single. Is this what you really want? Definitely not! If it were, your title would be "swinging single"—or "sincere single." First of all, to be swingless is not all that bad—especially when you match it against the swinging single who might be known for her frequent forays into erotic love affairs.

Most important is getting you off the shelf and into the main aisle of accessibility—whether it be dating, dieting, or doing your own thing.

Your prime target at this point is to get rid of negativism. If you say, "It's no use," it probably isn't. Instead, ask, "What's apt to be in it for me?" There can be laughter, love, and excitement never experienced before, because you haven't cut the negative strings that have tied you to solitude. As for the "I'll never get married" part—maybe not, maybe so.

Take stock right now and list what you do have to offer. List five areas that interest you. They may include hobbies, sports, politics, conservation, etc. After taking time to consider your interests, get involved with some activity. If you sew, make an inexpensive outfit for a needy child. Learn to play tennis or golf. Join an environmental-protection group. Remember the good feelings you experience as you take part in whatever activity you choose.

Perhaps you are one of the singles who say, "Why can't people realize that I just want to be left alone?" People probably don't realize why because they don't see satisfaction within you.

Our society demands a certain amount of socializing. When a person sees another person left out, his first response is to get him or her involved—especially if his life appears dull.

If you desire to be left alone, then in some way exemplify this way of life and let it reveal to others that not only do you have it all together but that you're satisfied with what you've got.

Perhaps you are the professional person who feels flopped on the shelf. You might say, "What they say is true. A middle-class black female gets a top job. Five years ago it was a middle-class white female, and before that, mainly middle-class white males. Progress maybe—but not fairly." Get off the shelf and speak up. Let the city, county, and state governments hear from concerned Christian women. Our country is going through an upheaval in restructuring government as well as business. If you feel there are unjust job placements, then you are probably the best one to speak about the issue. "The wheel that squeaks gets the oil."

The *Los Angeles Times* recently reported that the Los Angeles County government is desexing job titles. The woman who has been saying, "It's discrimination to be called a chairman when I am very definitely a woman!" should take heart, at least if she is in Los Angeles County.

There is to be a desexing of 170 job titles affecting the county's 81,000 employees. A fireman will become a fire fighter. A patrolman will be called a patrol officer. A kennel-man will be known as a kennel attendant. The pest control-man will be known as a pest-control worker, and, would you believe, a waitress will become a dining-room server!

Is a title all that important? Or is the personhood of the individual the primary point of our concern?

"It's not fair. The man next to me makes three thousand dollars more a year than I do and gets an additional week of vacation—would you believe we do the same type of work?" Another complaint surfaces as the Women's Liberation Movement goes forward with new legislation each month to insure women of their rightful wages.

But for God's woman shouldn't there be other priorities for equality? In some ways, yes. God's woman is sensitive, loving, at peace with the world, joyful, patient, kind, good, faithful, gentle, and filled with self-control. Her salary should be at least equal to that of any man doing the same job. She should also have the same opportunities. If a woman has entered the professional world, it is her obligation to get off the shelf and speak for equal pay, equal time, and equal opportunity. Radical? Not really—just getting proper compensation for equal contribution.

For all the battles and gains that have been won by professional women, there's still an unresolved tension when the working woman is also a homemaker and mother.

Probably the most frequently heard cry among these mothers is, "Sorry, I can't come over now. I just picked the baby up from the nursery school and since I only get an hour and a half a day with her I'd better stay home." The professional wife, mother, and worker has a heavy load to carry mentally and physically. A woman should carefully consider all the demands of a job outside the home before she decides to take one. She must ask herself what the reason is for accepting a job. If money is not a necessity, and since the first seven years are the most crucial for the social, intellectual, and emotional development of a child, will the added income balance out the lack of time spent developing the talents of her children? Single parents, however, may find it financially necessary to be employed. By carefully using the time that is available to them for rearing their children, however, single parents in many cases may avoid the developmental pitfalls that "absent" parents often encounter.

Many women who are maintaining these dual roles feel shelved and cheated of the day-to-day joys of caring for children, chatting with neighbors, and creating wall hangings. If you are on the shelf because of professional problems, get off! Move out to do something about those problems.

The moans of motherhood have been increasing with the development of labor-saving devices and the voices of feminists planting dissatisfaction in the minds of many women.

"No one ever told me it would be this much work to be a mother." This woman has placed herself on the shelf without looking beyond the work load. Yes, it is a lot of work to be a mother, and if the children are drawn into household tasks they will learn it is a lot of work *before* they take on a family responsibility when they get older.

My husband told me not long ago that our oldest daughter, before saying her prayers, said, "Dad, Mommy sure does a lot of work to make things nice for us, doesn't she?" Wow! She *has* noticed! I have attempted to bring the children to accept household responsibility because they are a vital part of its smooth functioning. But I have also tried not to overburden them. When I am getting ready for a speaking engagement or completing a manuscript I need time for myself. They realize this. They also know that the honorarium I bring home will be used for the Lord, for our living, and to provide a special time together. I believe that inactivity is an indignity of life. When we lose our motivation to work, we lose a certain self-respect.

This does not eliminate the fact that there is the feeling that I'll never catch up. I probably won't. Since I have realized this fact, I take more time with the children and I'm able to do more things I want to do and not let my need to get *all* things done frustrate me.

"What's wrong with me? Mrs. Lee is always so organized." Some women are, while others find they can never keep things out of the kitchen sink. If organization is what you want then get off the shelf and get organized. Make lists of priorities. What would you like to get done—today, this week, next month, or within the year?

It is nice to have a clean house. I love it but sometimes it's impossible. Seventeen years ago I tidied and dusted at night and in the morning. Oh, boy! I wonder how many other brides have done that. But not now! I started to change after a cousin visited us and later told me, "We loved our visit with you but we had hoped to just enjoy you. It seemed you were always keeping things so clean and neat! We didn't want that. We came to be with you and to enjoy being together."

I realized I had made them uncomfortable—the last thing I wish to do to anyone. So what do I do about my neatness problem? I keep a basic organization of each room and let the clutter fall where it may. Sometimes everything falls everywhere.

A woman can place herself on the shelf by being too organized as well as not organized enough. Undoubtedly, most women will have to choose between fastidiousness and fun. I have chosen general neatness and more fun because my children have so few years at home. If God has set me as an example for my children then they need to have access to me.

"Sorry, I can't come. I never seem to have time to go anywhere but the market, the vet, the dentist, the doctor, or the drugstore." Poor girl. She certainly isn't helping with the energy crisis. Her life is so busy it's difficult to believe she is able to visualize herself as being on the shelf—but she is. She is cheating herself of some of the greatest opportunities with her children. By using a calendar to organize appointments to coincide or to be consecutive, a woman should be able to attend a special function to please herself.

Every trip in the car can be a learning experience for one of any age. A preschooler can learn from his mother about cars, trucks, transporting of food, and traffic patterns. While sitting in a waiting room, the mother can reinforce learning by recalling what was seen by drawing a signal, and discussing its colors and what they mean. On the way home they can sing or laugh at something funny along the road. For the school-age child there can be the reinforcing of subjects learned at school. Isn't applying intellectual concepts to everyday life what gives life greater meaning?

Are we not more than parents? Yes—praisers, pleasers, and pushers. We need time with our children and traveling can provide a good opportunity for this. If the child is going to the doctor maybe he is experiencing fear or anxiety. What a wonderful opportunity to relieve anxiety before the experience. If the child is an adolescent, this opportunity to be together could be the event of the week. The busy lives led by members of this age group require their minds and emotions to be active a good part of the time. So when the chance is used to discuss a concern or a revelation, it brings the young person a feeling of being cared for on a more mature level.

If you choose not to go to a meeting because of an appointment or responsibility with your children, put your priorities in order. Before you jump off the shelf to take them someplace make sure you do it for the right reasons and that others know this is a special opportunity you will be sharing with your child.

"Go watch TV. I'm too busy." How many mothers are aware of television content? Why do you think the public is protesting about certain programs to the Federal Communications Commission? I have talked with a number of mothers who at one time or another have let their children randomly watch TV in order to do housework. Sometimes it was a selfish way of gaining a chance to just sit without entertaining Junior.

After glancing at the television one day, one mother exclaimed, "I couldn't believe that I saw a woman seductively dancing before a man on a popular children's program. Then I really came unglued when a half hour later my child started dancing that way in front of her daddy." And there is more. What about the cartoons where one character is stabbing the other in the back and blood spurts out like a fountain? That's a lot for a three- or four-year-old to handle.

As you sit on the shelf wondering how you can get the

kids out of your hair, analyze a few facts. On the average we have our children with us for 18 years. That means they are with us 6,570 days, totaling 157,680 hours. But that does not count the hours they are in school—that's if they were with us continually. If an average night of sleep is 8 hours (and it's more for children) then that takes away 52,560 hours and leaves us with 105,120 waking hours. To show what a small amount of time we have to teach, train, and love our children, consider the statistics for a person who lives to be 70 years old. He will live 25,550 days compared to those 6,570 days between birth and the age of 19. You only get him for one-fourth of his expected life span—and during the most formative years at that!

Now get off that shelf and enjoy those blessings!

The moans of motherhood will not stop just because I write about it or you stop moaning. In our accepting ourselves, just as we are, we can become what we ideally are capable of becoming. What our children become is apt to be a reflection of us. We will get back only what we give.

The self on the shelf is not apt to be there long if she starts where she is and recognizes her need to emerge.

3
The Need to Emerge

Oh, God, can't you see? I've got to be me! Free to be mentally, emotionally, and spiritually independent. Free to explore new avenues of thought. Free to respond at emotional levels beyond those of the children, free to have time with You. I'm not complaining, God, really I'm not, but I never have a moment to myself. I guess I've been on the shelf, but I want to get off. I need to emerge into a life that has greater dimensions. Help me to not let these feelings upset my family; but instead show me how I might become more informed, freer to express my individuality, and at the same time to be the efficient, organized, loving wife and mother that I know You intended me to be.

Just the other day a woman came to me in an almost apologetic way and said, "I am so frustrated and tired of the conflict I feel that I wonder if life will ever take on a peaceful, positive approach again."

Another woman recently said, "I have studied the Scriptures, attended meetings on becoming God's woman, and have felt truly satisfied with my life, but in all honesty there is something missing and as a Christian I am mystified. What has gone wrong? Why do I feel spiritually in tune and at the same time feel lacking as I attempt to face the world?"

There is nothing wrong with the concerns of these sincere

women. Through the past one hundred years, they have been seeking something more than being "just a housewife." Unfortunately, our society has failed to recognize the requirements for a good wife and mother. Because she has been "wageless," she has been relegated to the ranks of slavery. How sad it is to see women discounted when in truth we can be a dynamic resource.

For more than one hundred years our society has treated various aspects of womanhood unfairly. In some areas, women are justified in their demands for change: they have the right to resent being considered sex objects, just as they have the right to demand the same salary that men receive for the same job. But when it comes to equal rights in the home with a fifty-fifty work load between husband and wife, or to support abortion clinics and do-it-yourself pelvic exams, I think women united for these trivial causes are going a bit far. Feminists are also seeking to institute twenty-four-hour day-care centers. For a woman having a difficult time supporting children by holding down a job this would be a real boost. But when some are talking about total sexual freedom we find ourselves defeating the cause of the original Women's Rights Movement of the 1830s.

Sarah Grimké, the daughter of a slaveholder as well as a Quaker minister in her own right, addressed a letter to Mary S. Parker, president of the Boston Female Anti-Slavery Society, on July 11, 1837. It read, in part:

. . . . We must first view woman at the period of her creation. "And God said, Let us make man in our own image, after our likeness; and let them have dominion over the fish of the sea, and over the fowl of the air, and over the cattle, and over all the earth, and over every creeping thing that creepeth upon the earth. So

God created man in his own image, in the image of God created he him, male and female created he them." In all this sublime description of the creation of man, (which is a generic term including man and woman,) there is not one particle of difference intimated as existing between them. They were both made in the image of God; dominion was given to both over every other creature, but not over each other. Created in perfect equality, they were expected to exercise the viceregence intrusted to them by their Maker, in harmony and love. . . .

Here then I plant myself. God created us equal;—he created us free agents;—he is our Lawgiver, our King and our Judge, and to him alone is woman bound to be in subjection, and to him alone is she accountable for the use of those talents with which her Heavenly Father has entrusted her. . . .

Thine for the oppressed in the bonds of womanhood,

Sarah M. Grimké

Women were feeling the need to emerge in the time of Sarah Grimké. Their emergence included a sovereign God whom they realized demanded their individual accountability. Why should it be different now?

As we recognize our need to emerge into a larger sphere than our own little world the first premise is that in all things we must glorify the Lord. As we discover parallels between ourselves and the feminists of yesterday and today we must ask, "Does this particular attitude or action glorify God?" If so, then we have an equality which gives us the right to seek change.

We need to emerge from our own world into the world

that encompasses real and major problems. In the process of emerging we are going to discover a need to change. This could mean a change in our life-style, in our routine, in our attitude, or in our profession. To emerge might mean quitting a job to be at home, or possibly finding a part-time job to fill a newly recognized need.

I sent out a questionnaire in preparation for writing this book. From responses, I found that some professional women who have worked from the time they got out of high school or college wish they could be liberated from their jobs. They want to be home with their children and do a few creative things not associated with their work. Maybe this is typical of professional women. Sometimes the grass seems greener on the other side, doesn't it?

Millions of women are happy with their lives as home-makers, however, and other millions are satisfied and delighted to be career persons.

There are women who must work to earn money, while others work to fulfill personal needs. Whatever the reason or need, count the cost!

One of the disadvantages of being a working mother is running the risk of losing identification with sons and daughters. I've seen instances where, because the mother has been unavailable, the child gradually develops traits of destructiveness, lying, and stealing. For some reason the child seems to have an absence of guilt—an inability to discern right from wrong.

Some educators say that children having the greatest obsessions with their own bodies are those who come from broken homes or homes where the mother is frequently gone. Educators call this "separation anxiety." It is marked by discontinuity of a relationship between parent and child. Once this takes place it is difficult for the child to feel free to discuss even everyday matters with the parent.

While teaching at a school on the East Coast I observed a child on the playground during recess who continually masturbated. When I inquired about him I was told that his mother, who was divorced, had been contacted and she said that she would see what she could do but was too busy at the moment. This is not a universal problem for children of broken homes or for full-time working mothers. But an attitude of neglect can be destructive in many cases.

A disadvantage for the working mother, especially if she is working to supplement her husband's income, is that the money she thinks she is gaining she may in reality be losing. Most women who take jobs to supplement a man's income do it for the "extra"—another car, a lavish vacation, up-to-date appliances, or a new color television. But consider how the woman's salary must be divided up: "quickie" suppers to save time, child care, social security, taxes, extra transportation (taxi, subway, bus, gas), possibly a second car (tax, insurance, license), extra clothing in order to be in style, plus additional state and federal income taxes. After all that, it's questionable whether the woman's salary adds that much to the man's.

I know couples who both work. One woman feels it is essential even though her husband is making a sufficient salary. Now they have some extras. They take a month's vacation every year and go to plays, concerts, and amusement centers. It is also an interesting point that they don't attend church anymore because it just happens to come at the time they are leaving to go out for the day.

Lack of companionship with husband and family is another disadvantage for the working woman. Before work she is in a hurry and can't spend those extra moments soothing a child's uncertainties. In the evening, she is often too late or too tired to prepare a special dish for the evening meal.

After work she may be too exhausted to entertain or do anything more than grocery shop or maintain the house. Secretly, to make up the deficit in the lack of companionship, she buys gifts for her children. This satisfies her needs and takes away her guilt for not spending more time with them. But it does nothing for the children—except spoil them.

I used to be amused on the first and fifteenth of the month when I was in a toy supermarket and watched the number of parents buying basketfuls of toys for their children. Occasionally I would ask, "Are you getting ready for a birthday . . . or shopping early for the holiday season?"

The response was usually, "No, they've been good kids and since we just got paid we thought we would take them home a little something extra."

Fifty dollars for a good-behavior treat?

Also, working mothers of young children lose the opportunity to be on hand to answer important questions. This can bring about a breakdown in comradeship. "Why did my dog die?" "Where are the clouds going?" "Where does God live?"

One night when I was putting Timothy to bed I casually asked, "What makes you so sweet?"

With a smiling face and sparkling eyes he said, "Jesus. He's in my heart . . . but He's trying to get out."

"Why?" I asked.

"Because Jesus doesn't like to be in all that blood—does He?" answered Tim with a wrinkled nose.

There I was. If I hadn't been able to tell him that God didn't jump into his heart but was someone who loved him, would he have gone on thinking that Jesus was trying to get out of his little heart? What a marvelous chance for a mother to enter into the vast realm of her child's inquisitiveness!

Each woman must decide what's best for her and her family. It is no easy decision. Thought and prayer are needed to yield a satisfying answer.

We all recognize a need to emerge sooner or later. The width and breadth of that emergence is dependent upon our inner needs, arising from childhood experiences and developing to the present day.

As we emerge, our eyes must not rise to such worldly heights that our selfhood becomes unrecognizable. Instead, we need to make the marquee and see ourselves as lights drawing the world into the drama of God's love.

4

Making the Marquee

After my realization that I still had a long way to go down life's liberated road, I felt emotionally washed out. In fact I felt downright weak. I didn't feel any real joy and the only peace I felt was exhaustion.

I have a new love for my husband—for the patience he showed. I have a deeper understanding of my children—they have sensed my inner struggle. They have been trying very hard not to argue, to pick up their belongings, and not to insist on anything special. This means I must try even harder. I see they are putting into effect lessons I have attempted to teach them since infancy. Now when I hit a low period their lives exemplify my teachings. It's interesting that (as I hear them working in the kitchen) they say, "Please try to eat nicely," or, "Let's all work together so no one has to do it all." I appreciate that.

Part of the lesson I have learned in going through this inner strife is that anything worthwhile just might take a long time to accomplish. I am in no hurry, for I have lessons to learn, and what I learn I want to share.

I learned one particular lesson when I saw life as a theatrical stage and freedom as one of the characters.

The theme of the drama is the Creator and His goodness and love for man. God is on center stage beckoning each of us to enter—but we find our legs won't move. We watch. We think. And then we run to the wings. No, He isn't calling *me!*

Is He?

In the Garden of Eden a law was in force: "Thou shalt not eat of the forbidden fruit" (*see* Genesis 2:16, 17). Undoubtedly, Eve felt oppressed. Why shouldn't she be free to eat what she desired? After all, a friend, a questionable one for sure, had told her how good it would be. She had never known any difference until she was shown "something better." Eve became emancipated. But when God called her to center stage she hid. And what did He discover? Her emancipation was immersed in sin.

Some may say, "I've had enough of what the Bible says," or, "None of that stale material for me. The church is falling apart—I want nothing to do with it. I'm happy the way things are now."

Are you really? What about the people around you? What if you had seen me when I was struggling with my identity? The truth of the matter is that none of us is absolutely sure. We only feel secure or insecure, bonded or free.

How free are you? Is your body relaxed, your mind revitalized, and your soul refreshed? Do others bring you joy, or are they a bother or a burden? Do you spend more time praising good things or are you a faultfinder? Look carefully. Are you looking at life through glasses shaded with self-pity? For seventeen years I felt I was liberated. I thought I had conquered all those hang-ups other women have.

Remember that center stage? Are you ready to walk out on it—or are you heading for the wings?

Unfortunately too many of us find ourselves saying, "Next year things will be different. Next year. . . ."

What is total satisfaction?

Maybe it is having your name in marquee lights like Marilyn Monroe, Janis Joplin, or Jimi Hendrix. Maybe it is the success of playwright William Inge. What about the successful doctors, lawyers, and psychiatrists who, like the above, have met tragic deaths? No matter how popular or successful you are, you face death alone. We may run to the wings because "this God bit is a cop-out." Who can prove it really is?

What about reported healings, visions, and revelations? Are the individuals who are involved ready to be institutionalized, or is there truth to the reports?

Movie stars and professional people not only claim to have found freedom; they live as though freedom had found them.

Barbra Streisand stated in *Life* magazine:

> I don't understand the obligations of being a "star." I still can't understand the rumor and gossip market, distortions in the press, the intrusion on privacy. In my professional life, I am willing to be judged; my work is available for closest scrutiny. But my private life is my own, my most prized possession. . . .
>
> I look forward to working less and simplifying my life, to fulfilling some of my potential as an individual and as a woman. My little girl fantasy of being a recording star, a theater star, a concert star and a movie star is impossible to maintain; each of them suffers. There is so much else to learn, so much more to do. What I'd like is more time—time not only to read the stacks of political journals that have been piling up, but also time to read *Good Housekeeping* to find out different ways to decorate my son's sandwiches.

Dale Evans Rogers writes in *Time Out, Ladies,* "Life is pretty important: we only live once on this earth, and when that's over, it's over—so, . . . we'd better make the most of it while we've got it."

Dale, a star in her own right, has known insecurity, depression, vanity, and frustration. She lived for many years as a nominal Christian. It wasn't until her son, Tom, spoke to her about her spiritual condition and asked her to commit her life to Jesus Christ that her life became exciting. She says:

> He [Christ] is wonderful to me. He is my whole life, my prime reason for living, for keeping on even when everything seems to be going against me. He is wonderful to me because He is the fleshly manifestation of the fullness of the glory of God reborn within me. He has touched my life with His glory: I need no further "evidence" of His deity and power. I know, because I have experienced it.

Dale explains what being a Christian is like:

> Christ has given me a peace that the world does not understand and cannot supply. He has given me a very full cup of life since that wonderful day when I invited Him into my heart—a cup of happiness, of sorrow, of purpose, of challenge—and along with these things always His peace that the world cannot take away, regardless of its attacks.

Any woman who has freedom of spirit and the ability to accept not her will but the will of her Creator is truly a liberated woman.

I believe Dale's words. I always have, but somewhere

along the line I failed to learn a very basic lesson for liberation—to be liberated is to be continually learning.

Anna (*see* Luke 2:36–38), a religious woman, fasted and prayed night and day. In an age when women were old at thirty and were living on borrowed time at forty, Anna at eighty-four must have seemed timeless to the people who saw her sitting in the courtyard.

Anna did not romanticize life. Neither did she let on about any sorrow or loneliness she felt. Her trust in God's grace kept her from succumbing to despair. We all must play the waiting game at some time in life. We all must wait for something to happen—a promotion, a birth, or a death.

Anna was waiting for someone. She knew in her heart that something was going to happen. Not until many years later did she know what it was. Anna was eighty-four years old when Jesus was presented to the Lord. She witnessed His presentation. As she saw Mary and Joseph bring Him forth, she burst into praise for the fulfillment of the divine promises.

Anna had the will to live because she knew the power of God. She did not allow the culture of the times to depress her or make her feel she was not a part of society because she was a widow. She found a place for herself in the courtyard. It was a place where people could see, a spot where cantankerous citizens could witness the depth and peace of an old woman's life.

Anna had placed herself on center stage early in life. She had the courage to say, "Not my will, but Thine be done" (*see* Matthew 26:39). Anna was allowed to grow old gracefully and to witness God's glory made manifest in His Son.

If you find that the years are getting shorter, be patient. Put away self-pride and pity. Head for center stage. God is calling you. He has given each of us a certain number of years on earth. The day will come when we will be lifted off the stage of life and placed in the Hall of Eternity. Only the Director is able to withdraw us from the cast. But the person on center stage must fulfill the role the Director demands.

Christianity is not an escape route from life's problems. It takes courage to commit your life to Someone who can't be seen. Stop fighting for freedom! See freedom in Christ! And when you find it—float freely, unencumbered with trivialities.

Sarah, in the Old Testament, was called to center stage when the angel revealed to her the forthcoming birth of her child. At the time, according to the Book of Genesis, she was about sixty-five years old.

Sarah, whose name means "princess," was intelligent, opinionated, courageous, and liberated. As a young girl she was a socialite. She had a mind of her own. Yet, she was a selfless person.

The account in Genesis reveals that Sarah was a half sister to Abraham, but this had no serious effect on their marriage relationship. In fact, it worked to their advantage. Abraham recognized Sarah as his equal, yet each had a unique and satisfying role to play.

Abraham and Sarah dearly loved each other. In fact, Sarah wanted to please her husband so much that she gave him a woman, Hagar, so that the servant woman might present him with a son! What love! What liberation! Today such an arrangement would be considered a form of free love. Not then; it was an accepted act.

The love between Abraham and Sarah increased through the years. The miracle in Sarah's life, Isaac's birth long after she had passed the childbearing years, could occur only after she had accepted as her theme song "Is anything too hard for God?" (Genesis 18:14). She was called to center stage, where she found the Director dealing with her life in a miraculous way.

Sarah first had to allow God to have His complete will in her life. Could this mean that Abraham's first son, Ishmael, mothered by Hagar, was born because Sarah did not turn to God first in her frustration? If she had, possibly she would have known His original, unaltering plan for one man and one woman to be as one flesh.

If we do not wait on the Lord we create accidental problems—we get Ishmaels instead of Isaacs.

As I think about being God's liberated woman I am reminded of the Last Supper and the liberation Jesus gave to His disciples, especially Judas.

The banquet table is prepared for us. The host, Jesus, is accommodating. Spread before us are the ingredients for peace, purpose, and prosperity—prosperity in the true spiritual sense.

No advance reservations or tickets are needed. All we must do is prepare ourselves by saying, "I wonder what excitement lies ahead when I enter the banquet room?" No telling.

There is nothing we can do to elevate our worth or the place where we will sit. The entire banquet is unmerited. We are the guests—our only responsibility is to accept. If we refuse the invitation, though, there will be no hurt feelings —only disappointment on the part of the Host. There may be future invitations, but they are not unlimited. How many invitations will it take for us to say, "I accept"? How many before it's too late?

Some always find an excuse: "I don't want to be obligated." "I don't have time." "I don't need anything more.

I'm fine." "I don't believe that coming to Jesus can give freedom."

If you are too self-confident or overconfident, you are apt to be unaware of your greatest inner needs. Second Corinthians 12:9 reminds us, "My grace is sufficient for you, for my power is made perfect in weakness" (RSV).

There are as many reasons as there are excuses for rejecting intimate fellowship with Christ. People read newspaper reports about some of the major denominations' declining memberships and finances. What they don't know is that most of the churches that are dwindling are the ones that have phased out emphasis on the personal need for Jesus. They have replaced this with committees, chairpersons, co-chairpersons, and drives. Other people feel they don't want to get involved with a church because they are not religious. Wasn't it the "religious people" who crucified Christ?

Yet, many believe in God; they believe all the orthodox things about Christ. But they refuse to enter center stage.

If you are fighting for freedom, consciously or subconsciously, locate the areas in your life where you are bogged down. Why don't you feel free? What could you stop doing that would make you more liberated?

We will make the marquee when we accept and experience the Director's demands and move to center stage. We will see the antagonist and protagonist working out the theme of life's drama. A changed attitude brings about a changed life.

5
Changed Attitude, Changed Life

Now what do I do? I thought I had everything so organized in my mind and my thinking and I was really satisfied not to do any writing or speaking but to devote myself 100 percent to my family. A letter arrived from a magazine asking me to do a story on my travels just as I was preparing to leave for Europe. They would like a little more information. Swell! I had just packed everything up and they wanted more! What to do? This meant I would have to unpack everything. But I couldn't! I promised God I would be a happy, contented, liberated wife.

I now recall my husband's words the night I was so upset: "God does not want you to give up but He desires you to relinquish your drives and your motives. Think how you might most effectively live and still have a role with women."

Maybe God didn't want me to give up all my ambitions. Could it be He allowed me to experience all this in order for me to see the real freedom I have? Is a changed attitude and approach to life all it takes to produce a changed life?

Many women have found the secret to discovering self. Others are frustrated. Not long ago I directed a one-day retreat for women. The two most popular workshops were on prayer and on being liberated. This was a church retreat. Women inside and outside of the church need something more than meetings and church services. Look at the women around you. Which ones are satisfied? Which are shy? Get to know them.

It is important to recognize the unhappiness so many women experience—as well as to know how to cope with it. Women have been dealing with the same problems for more than two thousand years.

Pick up a magazine and you're sure to find something in it about "frustrated womanhood." But what about women who are satisfied with their lives most of the time? What about those with rejoicing hearts, who wake up each morning to look at a bright, new day? They are so excited about their own possibilities they get goose bumps! Have you ever had that feeling? I have—recently. I believe I'm starting to get the message.

Not long ago in the *Los Angeles Times,* columnist Art Seidenbaum related the hardships modern women encounter. He compared the family of man to the ever-present family of women. Women are the heads of more than 90 percent of the single-parent families in the United States. Many of these are encountering financial difficulties: 60 percent of women heading up families are on welfare. Many are burdened with the emotional, physical, or psychological hardships a typical one-parent family faces.

Seidenbaum pointed out that if these same families were headed by men, 90 percent of them would have their family income almost doubled. He also observed that a child's sense of self-worth is dependent upon the parent's view of himself. The parent who brings in an adequate salary but is not around to raise the children loses their respect. And the parent who collects welfare may be teaching the child to accept handouts.

Not only does a woman in this situation have to take stock and possibly change her attitude, but society must alter certain policies before lives can be changed.

Brigitte Bardot feels she has the greatest possible freedom. She likes to change male companions. To keep the same one soon becomes a bore. She advocates abortion on demand and sexual freedom. But the truth finally came out in a *Parade* magazine interview, where she stated, "I am probably now ready to have an enduring relationship with some worthy man." Because she has admitted she has had a long list of failures, she knows that "women get more unhappy the more they try to liberate themselves and act like men." She is not changing her attitude. Instead she is only altering her approach.

We see a fight for freedom among our high-school and college-age girls. The girls attending the 1973 annual Girl's State mock government convention at Squaw Valley, California, demanded the legalization of prostitution. Their plank said: "We are hopeful that by establishing prostitution as a regular business we could control it by legal and medical restrictions."

Not a chance! The works of the flesh are no different today from what they were thousands of years ago:

> For we naturally love to do evil things that are just the opposite from the things that the Holy Spirit tells us to do; and the good things we want to do when the Spirit has his way with us are just the opposite of our natural desires. These two forces within us are constantly

fighting each other to win control over us, and our wishes are never free from their pressures.

Galatians 5:17

Moral temptations are no different today from what they were thousands of years ago:

When you follow your own wrong inclinations your lives will produce these evil results: impure thoughts, eagerness for lustful pleasure, idolatry, spiritism (that is, encouraging the activity of demons), hatred and fighting, jealousy and anger, constant effort to get the best for yourself, complaints and criticisms, the feeling that everyone else is wrong except those in your own little group—and there will be wrong doctrine, envy, murder, drunkenness, wild parties, and all that sort of thing. Let me tell you again . . . that anyone living that sort of life will not inherit the kingdom of God."

Galatians 5:19–21

Can you deny any of the above? Isn't that what our basic nature is like? No wonder we're grasping at whatever we feel will give us freedom!

Is your liberated sister who is a radical activist free of these moral iniquities? No, she is undoubtedly oppressed by her evil nature. We all have this fallen nature. The only way out is to allow Jesus Christ to liberate us through His love.

I am reminded of the story of a young girl who lived in a major red-light district. For some reason this conscientious young woman became a prostitute, and rented extra rooms in her house to tourists. While visiting with the tourists, she learned about the major events of the day. She had neither a radio nor a television set, so this was the only way she became informed.

On several occasions, visitors told about a group of God's people who were determined to take over the city where she lived. She believed in God and feared Him. Her religious background was the worship of other gods. She was an Amorite. These people worshiped Chemosh, a god whom they believed demanded the offering of little children as living sacrifices and who required believers to pass through fire as a test of loyalty.

One day two men came to her home seeking information —we might say they were laying the groundwork for a "crusade." The prostitute lived in a worldly, ungodly city. But when the two men came to her house of harlotry and revealed the plan for the forthcoming rally, she agreed to help.

This is the story of Rahab, told in the second chapter of Joshua in the Old Testament. She lived in Jericho at the time when Israel entered the land of Canaan. Rahab was faced with a difficult choice when she had to decide between fidelity to her country or faithfulness to God's desired claim on her life.

Joshua sent spies to search the land. They came to Rahab's house and had been there a short time when their presence was reported to the king of Jericho. " 'They are spies,' [the king] explained. 'They have been sent by the Israeli leaders to discover the best way to attack us' " (Joshua 2:1–3).

When the Israelite spies made the first visit to Rahab she said:

> I know perfectly well that your God is going to give
> my country to you. . . . We are all afraid of you; every-

one is terrified if the word *Israel* is even mentioned. For we have heard how the Lord made a path through the Red Sea for you when you left Egypt! . . . No one has any fight left in him after hearing things like that, for your God is the supreme God of heaven, not just an ordinary god.

Joshua 2:9–11

Rahab hid the spies in her house. Before she helped them escape from the city, she made them promise to spare her life as well as those of her relatives.

Can't you hear Rahab's mother prior to the battle? "Who, me? Go over to Rahab's house? I wouldn't be caught dead there!"

But if she hadn't gone, the mother would never have lived! It is recorded that all of Rahab's family went to the house of harlotry and after the battle they became Israelites and believers in Jehovah (*see* Joshua 6:25).

By faith—because she believed in God and his power—Rahab the harlot did not die with all the others in her city when they refused to obey God, for she gave a friendly welcome to the spies.

Hebrews 11:31

Joshua brought thousands of Israelites to Jericho and after seven days the walls came tumbling down. Joshua "fit de battle" of Jericho—and Rahab became a firm believer in God's power.

At last! Rahab was liberated not only from prostitution but also from an evil society—proof that a changed attitude brings a changed life!

58

Only one law can terminate prostitution—or, for that matter, lesbianism—the Law of the Lord: "Love the Lord your God with all your heart, soul, and mind." There is a second part: "Love your neighbor as much as you love yourself" (Matthew 22:37, 39).

> Come, let's talk this over! says the Lord; no matter how deep the stain of your sins, I can take it out and make you as clean as freshly fallen snow. Even if you are stained as red as crimson, I can make you white as wool!
>
> Isaiah 1:18

> Yes, all have sinned; all fall short of God's glorious ideal; yet now God declares us "not guilty" of offending him if we trust in Jesus Christ, who in his kindness freely takes away our sins.
>
> Romans 3:23,24

What tremendous news! But here's the greatest part: Rahab in her belief made the Israelites her people. She later married Salmon and became the mother of Boaz, the grandfather of Jesse. She thus became the mother of a long line representing God Himself: David, and one thousand years later, Jesus Christ.

Other women of the Bible such as Tamar and Bathsheba, who had been sinful, were also used by God.

Our past sins and our present situation do not matter to God if we are now willing to let Him mold our lives. We can have a dynamic purpose in this world if we trust the Lord.

Paul refers to Rahab as one of a "great cloud of witnesses" (see Hebrews 11:31; 12:1 RSV). Do you know any

"Rahabs"? How many women have the maturity to separate themselves from wrong associates in order to accept the gift of grace? Rahab made her home available and it changed her attitude and brought her salvation.

A couple of years ago a friend, Winnie Ingram, sent me a poem she was inspired to write after taking a desperate woman to church with her. She wrote:

> Today I invited a sinner
> to go to church with me,
> And there she heard the story
> of Jesus' love for thee.
> The burden she carries is heavy,
> she's lonely and in despair.
> I wonder how many Christians
> can truly say they care?
> My Jesus would not turn His back,
> nor utter words to crush,
> He would lift His eyes to heaven,
> and reach His hands to her in trust.
> Praise the Lord there were many like Him
> in church with me today,
> Who smiled to the sinner a warm welcome,
> and bowed their heads to pray.
> But sadly there were the few others,
> who lowered their heads in bold disgust.
> You see they knew the sinner,
> and spoke with memoir of her lust.
> Happily my humble, desperate sinner,
> she went to church with me. . . .
> She did not hear the hurting whispers,
> of those in sin like she.
> For God had guided her to come

to church with me and pray;
And there she heard only of His promise
   to love and help her find His way.
Oh, yes, my friend, there are tears
   which need to be wiped and dried.
And loving arms need to be outstretched,
   without that ugly pride.
So when my lonely sinner
   comes back to church with me,
May the gift of His salvation
   bring her hope and set her free.
And as her Christian sister,
   we'll pray her soul will find the rest,
And she will have a friend in me . . .
   as she's put to the daily test.
I'm glad I took this sinner,
   to church with me today.
For Jesus also touched my heart,
   and a rich blessing came my way.

Winnie was inspired to write this poem because her heart and soul had seen into the heart of a friend. I admire Winnie because she is an aspiring writer who isn't afraid to put pen to paper when she feels the urge. More important, she believes God uses her when she makes herself available. Once her attitude toward God changed, her life became dynamic. It is now a channel to tell others about an abundant and overflowing life filled with the riches of God's kingdom and the expectation that tomorrow will be another exciting day.

6
The Five Freedoms

As I find my attitude changing I feel the scope of my life expanding. I have been doing a great deal of reflecting. My lessons of liberation have led me to seek and set in cement five freedoms that are essential not only for my growth but for the enrichment of my children's lives and those of the people around me.

Several years ago a book titled *The Feminine Mystique* had women quietly talking about their roles in home and community. Today the whispers have become a roar. Through an assorted number of writings women have been made aware of their "oppressed condition." I have always asked, "What oppression?" But once again I have discovered certain truths to the feminist movement. I see these truths as resting on five basic freedoms. In each of these freedoms we should be able to recognize ourselves to some degree—what we have been, what we are, and what we hope to be. Some may discover through these five areas why it is difficult to change attitudes.

Each of us entered this world as a small, helpless mass of protoplasm and genes. Our parents nurtured and cared for us and we started to display characteristics—good and bad —of our parents. What we are now was most likely determined by how much freedom we had to grow up.

1. *Freedom to Grow Up.* Parents today are made aware of their great responsibility through reading newspaper and magazine articles as well as watching television talk shows and hearing conference speakers. We are able to gain much from outside information but it isn't until we take the tips and apply them that our children benefit from our learning.

The National Association for Mental Health states that a child's mental health is dependent upon the amount of love he receives, how he is accepted in the family, how secure he feels, and how protected he is. The association also says that every child needs some feeling of independence and a set of moral standards to live by. Guidance and discipline are required by every parent for each child in order for the child to learn right from wrong.

Freedom to grow up in a liberated family does not mean a child should be allowed to say anything at any time or place. A child-dominated family is anything but a liberated one, but self-expression can lead to dynamic dialogue.

If parents would firmly and objectively raise their children they would find mature adults twenty years later.

The Apostle Paul made this clear when he said, "Children, obey your parents; this is the right thing to do because God has placed them in authority over you" (Ephesians 6:1).

How do we obtain the freedom to grow up? We need to begin with ourselves: those fears, frustrations, and fantasies; the good and bad aspects of our own childhood; the hopes and dreams we have for the future.

The need to understand oneself can provide an opportunity for husband and wife to communicate—possibly for the first time in many years of marriage. The depth of oneself can best be discovered when the childhood years are relived. If possible, ask your parents about those early years

—are you able to recognize the instances of freedom you had to explore new avenues? Or, maybe you can see more clearly why you feel oppressed now.

Unfortunately, the age-old idea that little girls need dolls to be good mommies and boys need hammers to be successful daddies is a misconception. Men and women are capable of performing tasks generally assigned to the opposite sex. Being liberated is being able to do these jobs and maintain one's own individuality as well as one's sexuality.

When our family was going through a transition due to a move across the country we found our roles very mixed up. I'm sure that in the eyes of some of our Christian friends we were being antiscriptural. I was painting, landscaping, and making repairs. My husband would go to his new job, put in a full day of work, and come home after dark mentally exhausted. Anyone stopping by after he got home would find him helping with the dishes or bathing kids—maybe even vacuuming. By nighttime I was bone tired. He needed physical exercise so he helped me in the house. We needed to team up our efforts. We were doing what we could to help each other.

I find this to be quite a contrast to the thinking of those who believe you need to attend a dozen or so consciousness-raising group meetings in order to discover your liberated self. If these individuals—men and women—are so liberated because of these meetings why are they defensive about the need for them? Why do they continue to say, "We must be liberated"? Let's get on with it! To be liberated is to be free of something. I wish the consciousness raisers would spell out what that something is.

I am learning to be liberated. I have nothing to prove. I am me—a wife, mother, daughter, and sister—not only in a familial relationship but in a community sense. I can live only in interdependency with others. All women are my sisters because we have one Father. The differences among us are our choices of direction. Some are fighting for liberation from "whatever" and others have discovered a life of freedom through Jesus Christ. We are still sisters. The only difference is that attitudes haven't always changed in the right direction.

Not long ago I attended a National Organization for Women (NOW) rally. There were buttons for sale to identify each of us with the movement. I bought one that said SISTER. Did these women who were using four-letter words so fluently and sleeping with each other realize—or could they have understood—my interpretation of sisterhood? Don't misunderstand me. Several of my good friends belong to NOW and they are definitely not radical women, nor are they lesbians. Each chapter of the movement contains a uniqueness all its own.

The women I refer to (radical feminists) consider their sisterhood unique, something necessary for "the cause." There is also sisterhood because of God's grace, a bond of loving-caring that helps us share an experience. Christian women today are experiencing sisterhood in new ways. Small groups are emerging in almost every community— some for discussion relating to the woman's role in the home, church, and community. Other groups meet for Bible study and prayer. The experiences we share with others in small groups can aid us in developing the purest of relationships. Paul says, "Treat the older women as mothers, and the girls as your sisters, thinking only pure thoughts about them" (1 Timothy 5:2).

Freedom to grow up involves taking the ingredients of our childhood, mixing them with the good intentions of our parents, adding the staples of life, and letting them rise to fullness of stature. This recipe is a creative one because any of life's ingredients (experiences) can be added to enhance the flavor of the individual.

The greatest of all experiences is when we add up the sum total of life and realize that the greatest wealth will come when we seek our Creator through Christ the Liberator. And when children bless our lives we will have learned firsthand the importance of growing up—free to experience life and free to understand the feelings that give us the impulses to move ahead or wait patiently.

As liberated women we must not cheat our children of meaningful experiences. It is our responsibility to encourage them in nonsexist activities as well as to reveal to them the beautiful roles given to them because of their sexes.

I am reminded of David's words in Psalms 139:15,16: "You were there while I was being formed in utter seclusion! You saw me before I was born and scheduled each day of my life before I began to breathe. . . ."

2. *Freedom to Speak.* "What turns me on? Doing my housework in a bikini." That could very easily have been a reply to a newscaster on one of our nation's call-in shows. The radio broadcaster is penetrating the domain of the home to discover what is really on the minds of women. Washington, D.C. has "Confidentially Feminine," San Francisco broadcasts "California Girls," while Minneapolis boasts "Girl Topic." For some women this is a way to be heard; others believe it to be an invasion of privacy.

There are other ways to be heard. Phil Donahue, Mike Douglas, and Johnny Carson are among those who allow individuals to spout off or share their feelings on their television shows. There are magazines that have individualized serials relating things such as, "How to Be a Woman" and

"I Learned to Be a Mother After My Children Grew Up."

These means of self-expression are good. But what would happen if we started revealing some of these statements and stories to those living with us—to those who care? It is strange that people can write something for publication but when it comes to relating on a one-to-one level the brain dries up and the eyes become sullen.

I was impressed to learn about the relationship between Susan and Janet. Janet had always admired Susan because of her selflessness. Susan had been an honor student, a class officer, and generally, a nice girl. Her friend, Janet, periodically ran around with the more popular crowd but was also an individual. Janet had always tried to be friendly to everyone, but an inferiority complex kept her from realizing her potential. A few weeks prior to the five-year reunion of their class, Susan mentioned to Janet how much her friendship had meant. That one compliment gave Janet a new lease on life.

The case of Tom and Betty is another classic example of exercising the freedom to speak. Typical of many couples who have been married for a few years, Tom and Betty were in one of those "down" stages of their marriage—nothing serious, just a case of busyness. Tom had been having to do extra work at the office because of some late contracts and a month had gone by with erratic dinner hours and evenings that usually concluded with a big flop into bed. Betty was fine for the first couple of weeks but then she began to show signs of strain. She snapped at Tom about the most trivial matters or she became sarcastic. In addition, their son had broken his leg and she had to wait on him.

One night, Betty threw herself on the bed and had a good cry. As she reached for a tissue she saw a note written by her son: "I know you're tired, Mom, but I love you. My leg will be better soon and then I can help you. Good night. Your son."

As if jolted by an electric shock, she realized how life had gotten her down. She washed her face, combed her hair, and when Tom entered the room she said, "I know you're tired but maybe you could take a few moments to share ways that I could help you during these difficult days. I love you and appreciate all you do."

Fifteen seconds were all it took to save this marriage. It didn't cost a cent—only a little pride. Betty was heard, and the marriage is on solid ground. Their son had learned from their good example during his early years and now he had been the stimulus to healing in his parents' marriage.

It is difficult to start sharing feelings if this has not been done before. Don't expect too much of the nonresponsive partner and don't get discouraged if you find it difficult to express your own thoughts. Remember the changed attitude we talked about earlier? With that will come a more confident self and a relaxed way of expressing yourself.

There is much more to be said about communication and if this is a difficult area for you I recommend *The Miracle of Dialogue,* by Reuel Howe. It gets to the point and gives some constructive suggestions.

3. *Freedom to Wear a Label.* Did your children see Ms. Claus last Christmas, or was it Santa Claus? More than likely, it was good old Saint Nick.

In this day of Women's Lib, Western Girl, the third largest temporary-help service in the United States, sponsors a Santa division. It supplies "super Santas" to many of the nation's department stores. Two women trained to be "Santas." They were honor graduates. But they waited and waited to be called. The Christmas season came and went but there was never a request for Ms. Claus.

There's a lot in a label. Have you ever been puzzled by the title of a person? Not long ago I was required to respond to an organization. I was unable to obtain the president's name and did not know if "it" was a man or woman. I could have gambled and written, "Dear Sir," but if it were a woman she would have been offended, especially in this day when some people are so sensitive about titles. If I had known it was a woman, would I have addressed it "Dear Miss" or "Dear Mrs." or "Dear Ms."? I guess we'll always be safe in writing, "To Whom It May Concern."

Recently I have been receiving some mail addressed to Ms. Chandler. My daughter asked me, "Does that mean you're going to be going topless or marching in front of the White House?" She had been with me on several occasions to witness such feminist rallies. I readily observed how the liberationists' actions had spoken louder than their words.

What are we coming to? I want to be respected as well as respectful but what do I do if I don't know? I must remember to write Ann Landers about that.

Speaking of labels, what about the new vocabulary you need if you are attending conventions or meetings with Libber groups? Some of the major church denominations are going through a change in the same way. At several church conventions this past year, "Mr. Moderator" was replaced with "Chairperson."

"Ms." is being used by many companies in their correspondence, advertising, and literature. For some recipients this is avant-garde. Still, many resent having the *r* left out.

To add the *r* to Ms. is a sign of distinction. It represents the desirability of one person to another. There is the supposition that two individuals have the strength and stability to make a union, to be the responsible agents for future Americans. "Ms." or "Mrs." should carry respect and dignity. An individual should be free to make the decision relating to her title.

Personal titles are one thing; emotion labels are another. Are you moody, stressful, fatigued? To wear a label like that is definitely out for the liberated woman. If you are seeing yourself honestly and find you are presenting a negative impression, do something about it! Remember Christ's promise:

> I am leaving you with a gift—peace of mind and heart! And the peace I give isn't fragile like the peace the world gives. So don't be troubled or afraid.
>
> John 14:27

If you are moody, take a walk. Don't just sit there feeling sorry for yourself! If you are stressful, get rid of the stress. Change your routine, get out of your rut. Ask the family to do something out of the ordinary with you. Recognize the areas of stress. Make a list of those you can conquer and those that will require additional help. Take time to put your life in perspective and a new you will emerge.

Then there is that female dilemma of fatigue. Yes, it's real. It's not in your mind. But it can give you a label that says, "Oh, yes, Mrs. Jones is always so tired."

Some women go through periodic flirtations with fatigue. This is their nature. They go headlong into a project, pursue it, and then—wham! They're exhausted. They ache. Their head spins. They're irritable. All they want to do is sleep. It's a terrible feeling. (I know!) Then they take stock of the situation and realize what has happened. A few early-to-bed nights, a relaxed schedule—telling people no when they request personal services (selfish, yes, but sensitive and thoughtful to the family), and changing the family routine to insure getting out of the rut. Eventually a woman will find herself working harder and enjoying it more.

Voilà! A new you. However, there is one catch to this individual endeavor. It is possible only when you realize that the impact of the change comes when power from the Holy Spirit takes over all weakened areas. Remember the beautiful peace, the feeling of security that can be yours if you trust in Him. Take the opportunity—don't let it pass you by. This is when God will deal with you.

Are you wearing a label? What does it say? How does it contribute to the well-being of you, your family, and the community in which you live? It is also possible that a label may need to be replaced with a different title. Be sure of what your label says and then wear it with pride.

4. *Freedom to Be Employed and Educated.* "If only I could be liberated from this job! For once, it would be so wonderful if I could fulfill my dream of staying home . . . being a homemaker, mowing the lawn, wiping my kids' noses."

Does this sound like a liberated woman? She is the envy of many of her friends, yet she is oppressed by her career. She is a frustrated female because she accepted a job and is unable to justify a resignation. Incredible!

In several women's magazines I have been reading, women write about breaking out of the "home mold." It's ironic. Never satisfied, are we?

New horizons are opening up for women all over the country. Some women need to get out of the house. My only question is, "Why?" Will the end result justify the means?

To be a liberated woman is to be YOU—not what you think others want you to be, not what society says you should be—but YOU. Your abilities, ambitions, and aspirations are unique.

What is the real you? Take a few minutes to jot down some of your thoughts.

If you hear the call of the working force, do some exploring into the types of jobs available and your possibility of obtaining employment.

Today the woman exploring the availability of more education is most likely in her thirties or forties. She may want nothing more than to complete something she started a few years ago. Possibly her head was in the clouds and she wasn't doing well—marriage was an easy out. Now she has an insatiable desire to accomplish a goal—to contribute in some way to society.

Mary Lou, an attractive, athletic-type person, discovered a deep-down desire to return to college to obtain her master's degree in literature. At the time her boys were seven and ten years old and depended on her being at home before and after school.

After making some inquiries, she discovered that the master's program was possible and could be completed by taking one course a semester and one full summer session. She spread the program over several years and completed the summer-school program when the boys were older. She has been in an academic atmosphere for several years and now, with a master's degree, two well-adjusted boys, and a husband who encourages her, she is ready to move into the professional world.

Maybe you have been out of school for a long time and you lack self-confidence. Or possibly you never quite finished your degree. The University of Michigan made a study and discovered that married career women see themselves as better mothers than those who stay at home. They not only have intellectual stimulation through their jobs but also the satisfaction of being responsible for a family.

A number of colleges, universities, and private organizations sponsor special courses for women. Some offer tests measuring aptitude and ability as well as interests. Seminars, lectures, and personal counseling sessions are set up to offer the opportunity to become a professional person.

An aid to giving women insight before they break into the ranks of the employed is a pamphlet titled *Continuing Education Programs and Services for Women.* It may be obtained by sending forty cents to the Superintendent of Documents, United States Government Printing Office, Washington, D.C. 20402.

Another help: Many colleges and universities have a division of continuing education. Programs center around a life-planning process for women. They help women discover who they are, what they want to do, where they want to go, and how they want to get there.

The Miami-Dade Community College in Miami, Florida, has one of the most complete programs for women that I have discovered. In October 1965, the greater Miami area felt a need to delve into the subject of women and their specific needs. The Council for the Continuing Education for Women was formed and today it is a thriving institution. It sponsors E-V-E programs that deal with three approaches to women's needs: 1) Minifairs, which have display tables of literature and, often, representatives of the employment community. 2) My Fair Lady, a community-wide exposition for women. 3) Daytime seminars for women, held mornings and afternoons.

I mention these programs because I believe they can be

helpful. On the other hand, some aspects of these services can be detrimental if they overstress the importance of the woman as a career person. Use discretion and don't be too gullible.

Then there are women who stay at home and obtain their employment through free-lance work as salespersons, using the telephone, mailings, or door-to-door visitation. This can be a rewarding experience. I belong to those ranks, as a writer and speaker, but watch out—it can get you down. A woman must be well on her way to knowing she is liberated and knowing her do's and don'ts before she tackles home employment. She must be a disciplined person and have a well-defined schedule or her job may lead her to an intensly nervous situation.

In the final analysis, every advantage to working at home could be matched by a disadvantage. Only the person involved can make that decision.

Several years ago my husband (then self-employed and working at home) came into the kitchen and let out a groan. "What's the matter, dear?" I inquired.

He plopped into a chair, cradled his head on his arm, and said, "Dear, I have a bad case of inertia." That is a major disadvantage of at-home employment.

5. *Freedom to Run the World.* When feelings of restlessness or inadequacy creep into our lives we say, "What am I to do? Life is so rude. Nobody cares. I don't have time for anything anymore."

All too frequently we attempt to escape these negative feelings by becoming overly involved in civic or social activities. That may help others—but not you.

If we are to be leaders in the world we need power. When we are ready to yield ourselves to God's power, we feel the surge of His Spirit. He says, *You've got it, do it!*

At last we find a basic contentment. Our lives bear the fruits of the Spirit. We are at peace. Usually this comes after a reassessment of our lives—after taking inventory of our basic goals. It is personal and penetrating, something that can only be accomplished on an individual basis.

At times the old negative feelings will creep back. Don't let them overtake you. Remember Jesus' gift of peace of mind and heart. At other times you may slip into a reflective mood. Reality grips you and awareness of your lack of communication with God is evident. Get a grip on your emotional and intellectual faculties—and you'll be back on the mountaintop!

We have a mission. Yes, we are responsible for the organization and maintenance of this world. Why? Because we have the physical capacity to produce offspring and the mental fiber and emotional possibilities to teach and train them.

The YWCA, the stronghold for many women's and young girls' activities, has now become so actively involved in the Rights Movement that it will not discriminate on its governing boards, or its staff, against homosexuals. The Y decided that sexism was too deeply embedded in our society and it was time women were released from being programmed as nonpersons. In 1973 the YWCA called for low-cost abortions. They have also been changing their programs from cooking and sewing classes to consciousness-raising sessions for men. One chapter has a co-op for women who are obtaining their own divorces. The Y is not abandoning its old activities altogether—it wouldn't dare. But a Y ad makes me wonder about the real freedom from which an unsuspecting woman might be kept. It reads: ''Join the gentle explosion at, of all places, the YWCA.''

76

We need our individual freedom in each of the areas I have mentioned. But that freedom must have a source. Jesus said, "I am the Way—yes, and the Truth and the Life. No one can get to the Father except by means of me" (John 14:6).

We have the freedom to grow up, to expand our interests and intellect and pass on the breadth of that freedom to our children. We have the freedom to express ourselves. But only when our tongues are under the power of the Spirit will our words mean anything of value:

> So also the tongue is a small thing, but what enormous damage it can do. A great forest can be set on fire by one tiny spark. And the tongue is a flame of fire. It is full of wickedness, and poisons every part of the body. And the tongue is set on fire by hell itself, and can turn our whole lives into a blazing flame of destruction and disaster.
>
> James 3:5, 6

It is not strange that women desire to break out of "a mold." Isn't that the story of Original Sin? We are given the freedom to do as we please. But only when we claim the power of the Holy Spirit do we experience peace within ourselves. "I am leaving you with a gift—peace of mind and heart!" (John 14:27).

God has allowed us to become liberated so that we may have the freedom to choose our own labels. It is not only a "Ms." or a "Mrs."; it is how others see us. Because of this, it is important to remember:

But you are not like that, for you have been chosen by God Himself—you are priests of the King, you are holy and pure, you are God's very own—all this so that you may show to others how God called you out of the darkness into his wonderful light. Once you were less than nothing; now you are God's own. Once you knew very little of God's kindness; now your very lives have been changed by it.

1 Peter 2:9, 10

Christ gave each woman a new dignity. I recall how warm and patient He was with the inquisitive Mary, and how loving and tolerant of Martha's busy management of the house.

When Jesus came to the home of Martha and Mary, Martha was busy serving. Undoubtedly she had been working frantically and was getting desperate as the dinner hour approached. She said, "Lord, do you not care that my sister has left me to serve alone? Tell her then to help me."

"But the Lord answered her, 'Martha, Martha, you are anxious and troubled about many things; one thing is needful. Mary has chosen the good portion, which shall not be taken away from her' " (Luke 10:40–42 RSV).

As free women we can choose education, employment, or home economics, but only when we choose according to God's will does our task take on meaning.

7

Paul and the Liberated Woman

It's a warm afternoon on the patio. I am watching the precision of the hummingbird as it sucks nectar from the bottlebrush. He reminds me again of the lessons I'm learning each day: to be precise in all I do, to have a purpose for my life, to be a godly woman. And to be that type of woman I must deal with what the Bible has to say to me. How can its words have such an adverse effect on those engaged in the Feminist Movement?

Oh, God, I long to love You more intensely each day. I yearn to be an all-year channel for Your wisdom and love. Teach me from Your Word. Empower me to use it in my life for Your sake. Amen.

Every feminist seminar, rally, or convention I've attended has promoted basically the same idea, that women are finally going to achieve the position and prominence they deserve. That is also stated in the chorus of an ode sung about the feminists in Euripides' *Medea,* written five hundred years before the time of the Apostle Paul.

Women are no different today from what they were twenty-five hundred years ago. Women are the same as they were in the beginning. The difference is cultural behavior. Anyone who reads Margaret Mead's book *Male and*

Female will readily see that we are all born into cultural climates that aid in determining our roles and our responses.

The Women's Liberation Movement has been knocking on the door of the Church for many years. The major difficulty with admittance has been that the institutional Church has in some ways been too heavenly minded to be any earthly good.

During the time of Abraham, Solomon, and David, women were placed in the background and the men did the ruling. This tradition has been handed down in the Church through the ages.

Libbers have entered a hate campaign against the Apostle Paul because of his references to women in the New Testament. What they do not understand is that Paul is speaking partially from his own background in life. He did not walk hand in hand with the Man, Jesus. He did not sit in on conversations Jesus had with women, although he knew about them. He was aware of Christ's delegating authority to women. We cannot condemn Paul until all sides have been explored.

Paul had strong feelings about women and it is important to understand what he was attempting to say as well as the context in which he said it.

Silence, submission, and subjection had a place. They still do. But service and sincerety are of primary concern to Christian women today.

> Christian women should be noticed for being kind and good, not for the way they fix their hair or because of their jewels or fancy clothes. Women should listen and learn quietly and humbly.
>
> 1 Timothy 2:10, 11

Paul was writing against a dual backdrop of Jewish and Greek cultures. Jewish women were considered of low position. Men prayed in thanksgiving that they had not been made a Gentile, a slave, or a woman. A Jewish woman was at the disposal of her father or her husband; she had no rights of her own. In the synagogue, the men learned while the women listened. If a strict rabbi were to meet his wife or a female relative on the street, he would not greet her.

Greek women also occupied a lowly position, in fact, more lowly than that of Jewish women. Talk about oppression! Women today have nothing to complain about compared with Greek women in Paul's time.

In the Temple of Aphrodite in Corinth one thousand priestesses were prostitutes. A married woman lived in confined quarters. Only her husband was allowed to enter her chamber. A wife was the means to legitimate children.

As part of the Greek culture, women dressed elaborately. The Greek mystery religions frowned upon elaborate dress but women nevertheless liked ornate styles. Paul's remarks about jewels and fancy clothes were necessary because of the fads regarding women's wardrobes. Emphasis on finery was endangering the relationships of new Christians to Christ.

Many teen-agers get automobiles while in high school. Did you ever notice what often happens to their grades? They drop because of the added attention to the car. If Paul were speaking in this vein today, he could easily have spoken a warning to teen-agers about the dangers of overattention to cars.

Paul was not making a permanent rule. It was temporary because of the social conditions at Corinth. Today he might tell a new convert that Christian women should be noticed for being kind and good, not for wearing revealing clothes.

Women should listen and learn quietly and humbly and stand firmly for what they believe to be God's will in their lives and the world, remembering that Christ's message was that we (male and female) were created equal.

Paul's true view is found in Galatians 3:28: "We are no longer Jews or Greeks or slaves or free men or even merely men or women, but we are all . . . one in Christ Jesus."

Women will find life and salvation not in clothes or in meetings, but in motherhood and godly living. A woman can find the crown of life in motherhood.

"But there is one matter I want to remind you about: that a wife is responsible to her husband, her husband is responsible to Christ, and Christ is responsible to God" (1 Corinthians 11:3).

Responsible means to be able to answer for one's conduct.

Ed and Linda had been having some minor difficulties in their marriage for about six months when Linda was attracted to another man. It was nothing more than "I think I could go for him if I weren't married." But because of her sincerity to her marriage she shared these feelings with Ed. He understood—at first—and then Satan influenced his mind and he became suspicious of everything. He told his wife he could never trust her and wondered now if the marriage could go on. Linda, in an emotional and almost delirious manner, expressed her feelings and then fell asleep exhausted. As if by a revelation Ed found that he had renewed feelings for Linda. She became exciting to him and the marriage blossomed with a new brilliance. Only when Ed allowed himself to be responsible to Christ was the marriage restored.

The eleventh chapter of First Corinthians goes on to tell that a woman should keep her head covered in church as a sign of subjection to her husband. Once again, look at the context in which this was written. It had local and temporary significance.

A woman, when submissive to her husband, is anything but a weakling. To be submissive is to have the strength and maturity not to blow your lid but to support the authority God expects your husband to maintain.

In chatting with some women in the radical Feminist Movement I have learned that many, if not a majority of them, are divorced. They claim their husbands didn't care, worked late, spent long hours in bars, played golf all the time, or watched television all weekend. Some will admit that if their husbands had shown more interest or if they had been home more often things might have worked out. There are some women who are able to admit that a portion of the husband's problem was originally their (the woman's) insensitivity to assorted situations.

I believe women want leadership. It is from this base that their love can link up with their husband's leadership to build a lasting home and marriage.

Psychologists, examining the American father's role in the modern family, agree that many dads play a secondary role in decision making. This can cause a son to suffer. According to Dr. Henry Biller of the University of Rhode Island, boys who have disinterested or ineffectual fathers frequently grow up to be less masculine and less well adjusted than boys who have strong, reasonable, understanding fathers.

Regardless of the Christian concept, the man who takes charge of the household sets the stage for the development of leadership and love. The children and the wife as well as society gain strength. Each has a specific function and life moves on with a purpose. There is no dominance over each other. But the wife's submission of her love as an extention of Christ in her, and the husband being responsible to Christ and loving his wife as his own body, is God's perfect plan.

In the first century women were required to wear veils. It was a sign of being under authority. In oriental cultures, even today, the veil signifies power, honor, and dignity for a woman.

Corinth was a licentious city. Paul believed it was better to err on the side of being too strict than to err on the side of being too lax. A woman without a veil could have been considered "loose." Would this have been a good witness for a woman who had just become a Christian?

Although Paul stressed the subordination of women, he was emphatic about the partnership that is necessary between husband and wife.

> Women should be silent during the church meetings. They are not to take part in the discussion, for they are subordinate to men as the Scriptures also declare. If they have any questions to ask, let them ask their husbands at home, for it is improper for women to express their opinions in church meetings.
>
> 1 Corinthians 14:34, 35

It is difficult to rise above tradition. As I mentioned, Corinth had very lax morals. Paul did not want anything involving women to happen that would bring about false thinking, or even suspicion of immodesty. He placed great stress on proper behavior in church.

Paul recognized the individual gifts God had bestowed upon women, but he taught that they had to be used in connection with God's will for each individual.

I don't want you to get the idea that I am trying to justify Paul's ideas for his time only. His words are relevant today but they must be used in our cultural context.

Honor Christ by submitting to each other. You wives must submit to your husbands' leadership in the same way you submit to the Lord. For a husband is in charge of his wife in the same way Christ is in charge of his body the church. (He gave his very life to take care of it and be its Savior!) So you wives must willingly obey your husbands in everything, just as the church obeys Christ.

And you husbands, show the same kind of love to your wives as Christ showed to the church when he died for her, to make her holy and clean, washed by baptism and God's Word; so that he could give her to himself as a glorious church without a single spot or wrinkle or any other blemish, being holy and without a single fault. That is how husbands should treat their wives, loving them as parts of themselves. For since a man and his wife are now one, a man is really doing himself a favor and loving himself when he loves his wife! No one hates his own body but lovingly cares for it, just as Christ cares for his body the church, of which we are parts.

Ephesians 5:21–30

Paul is first telling us to submit to each other, not just socially over a particular issue but physically and intellectually.

A wife needs to respect her husband's leadership, because if he is showing her the same kind of love as Christ showed the Church (the love that led to His Crucifixion), then all of her desires and interests will be considered in his decisions.

Yes, this takes extreme Christian maturity. I am aware that not many possess it as completely as they should. But it is a goal and a lesson to be learned.

> (That the husband and wife are one body is proved by the Scripture which says, "A man must leave his father and mother when he marries, so that he can be perfectly joined to his wife, and the two shall be one.") I know this is hard to understand, but it is an illustration of the way we are parts of the body of Christ.
>
> So again I say, a man must love his wife as a part of himself; and the wife must see to it that she deeply respects her husband—obeying, praising and honoring him.
>
> Ephesians 5:31–33

A marriage is meant to last for life. It is the union of body, mind, and spirit for as long as the husband and wife live.

Divorce was becoming a fad in Paul's time. Paul became burdened by the ease with which a person could obtain a decree of divorce. What if he were here today?

At that time, although a woman could not divorce her husband for any reason, a man could divorce his wife for almost any reason at all! It is written in Deuteronomy 24:1, "If a man doesn't like something about his wife, he may write a letter stating that he has divorced her, give her the letter, and send her away." This was just a portion of the Jewish law regarding marriage and divorce.

A man seeking a divorce simply wrote, "Let this be from

me thy writ of divorce and letter of dismissal and deed of liberation, that thou mayest marry whatsoever man thou wilt." The letter was written in the presence of a rabbi and handed to the wife in the presence of two witnesses.

The women of Ephesus grew tired of this oppressive law. As a backlash, Jewish girls were refusing to marry. Women's Lib!

The law reached its peak of effectiveness. And then God sent His Son who liberated the marriage relationship. But there was one condition—the man had to head the household.

Paul firmly believed that love must be sacrificial, pure, unbreakable, and in the Lord.

Get acquainted with a couple, if you haven't already, who have a marriage based on God's love. They will admit there have been times when the relationship needed revitalizing. But chances are they will also tell you about the depth and the joys of their marriage.

There are other passages we could deal with but it is more important to understand the setting at the time they were written.

When Paul wrote his first letter to the Church at Corinth he anticipated Christ's return at any time. He wrote with urgency about the salvation of souls, and was little concerned about enduring personal relationships.

Nine years elapsed between that letter and the one to the Church at Ephesus. By then he realized that the Second Coming was further away than he originally thought and that marriage in Christ was a precious relationship. He drew numerous parallels between marriage on the human level and the "marriage" relationship of Christ and His Church.

Paul was a member of the Sanhedrin and a requirement

of membership was to be married. We know nothing of that relationship—if Paul *was* married—but we do know that he was not against marriage.

The Rev. William Barclay, a noted Scottish scholar and author, states in *Daily Bible Readings:*

> The husband is head of the wife—true, Paul said that; but he also said that the husband must love the wife as Christ loved the Church, with a love which never exercises a tyranny of control, but with a love which is ready to make any sacrifice for her good.

It is a sacrifice for a woman to be submissive to her husband, just as it is a sacrifice for a husband to refrain from exercising tyranny of control over his wife. That's a major lesson for liberated love!

8

The Hub of Happiness

Now if I'm becoming a more liberated woman and a better parent with a greater perspective, I need not only to schedule my time but also the activity time of my children. I see how my time with them, individually and collectively, not only aids me in recognizing their needs but also helps them to see that I am human and need their love and concern as much as they need mine.

I love the feel of accomplishment when, as a family, we can be of service to our church, school, or community. There are times God uses us as individuals on campus, at the office, or in the neighborhood. This means we are trying individually and as a family to nurture each other and those around us. In so doing, we are learning to carry greater responsibility.

Thank You, God, for making me a part of the hub from which happiness radiates. Lubricate my life with Your love and the power of Your Spirit so that I may never turn from You. Strengthen the spokes and make me a link of Your love so our family may do mighty works for You. Amen.

Although it is under attack from forces within and without, the home is the hub of the wheel that forms today's society. From this one location individuals reach into the community, county, and country—even the world!

As parents, we are the executive agents. Our attitudes, feelings, and perceptions determine the atmosphere of our homes. Children provide the pace that is usually kept. They are the "little us," regardless of what we want to think. As soon as they start school, they bring particles of emotion and education to us to enrich our lives—if we will accept them.

Visualize yourself, parent or grandparent, as the hub of a large wheel. The spokes leading from this hub are your children, grandchildren, and those whose lives you have touched. The rim is a surface that touches all of life. The chipped or cracked places are the areas of vulnerability, areas where you will be expected to respond.

A strong hub and strong spokes make it possible to repair the rim. But, if something happens to the strength of that hub, the wheel may have to be junked.

The Home as a Center for Meaningful Experiences

As I take a lesson from the Bible, I see vividly how the father is the leader and the mother is the link to every member of a liberated family. As the hub, the father and mother as a team should be strong. Their strength will come from the Creator, but only when they have yielded to Him.

A man takes his leadership position when he decides to "leave his father and mother, and be forever united to his wife. The two shall become one—no longer two, but one! And no man may divorce what God has joined together" (Matthew 19:5). What a responsibility! Jesus implied that when a man becomes mature enough to take a wife he has no need for control from his parents. He owes them respect, but he is now in control of his own household.

The key to a strong family is a strong father, secure in his leadership role. He is in charge of discipline whenever he is at home, and in the final analysis he makes major decisions. This does not mean that he turns a deaf ear to his wife's wishes, or that he rides roughshod over family feelings. He must be a sensitive, loving leader, but he should firmly take charge, as chief executive. According to the biblical pattern, he is to be the material and spiritual provider of the household—with rare exceptions. The wife is his counselor, confidante, and adviser, but she leaves the final decision solely in his hands. Her primary role—and one of the toughest to perform successfully day in and day out—is to set the spiritual tone and generate the proper attitudes in the home.

I know several couples who have made all of their decisions as husband and wife. There have been differences of opinion but in the final analysis decisions were made together. God grants this equality to husband and wife, but if a compromise or joint decision cannot be reached, the husband is the one to make the final choice. And if that choice proves to be wrong—have a great, big kiss waiting when the realization hits!

The mother is the link of love. She is responsible for maintaining the household her husband provides. Her maintenance is more than material—she must provide love. She should be available when the children come home from school. She may not know what has taken place in the life of her child, but willingness to listen may be the key to a child discovering a solution to a problem. When the father comes home from work, he needs a haven where he may rest and a place to find understanding and peace.

Some of my liberated sisters say of the life of such a wife,

"This is oppression." No; this is the freedom of love. Paul tells us:

> . . . husbands should love their wives as their own bodies. He who loves his wife loves himself. For no man ever hates his own flesh, but nourishes and cherishes it, as Christ does the church, because we are members of his body.
>
> Ephesians 5:28–30 RSV

We're not talking about an ego trip but secure feelings about ourselves.

Long ago a question was asked that has been repeated through the years: "How does a man become wise?" The answer was, "The first step is to trust and reverence the Lord!

"Only fools refuse to be taught. Listen to your father and mother. What you learn from them will stand you in good stead; it will gain you many honors" (Proverbs 1:7–9).

The father who has no authority has not earned respect. He has not set his eyes on the right goals.

The mother's position in the family carries the wonderful responsibility to train her children, to nourish their bodies, and to pour love into their hearts verbally and physically.

God commissioned parents. He promised them that "preaching will bring fathers and children together again, to be of one mind and heart, for they will know that if they do not repent, I will come and utterly destroy their land" (Malachi 4:6).

We were never promised there would be no "generation gap." Undoubtedly, there has been one since the beginning of time. The only difference now is that we have come up with a name to make a bigger wedge. I recall how Absalom became haughty and revolted against King David, his father (*see* 2 Samuel 14–18). In the New Testament we are told the story of the Prodigal Son (*see* Luke 15:11–32).

Paul was sensitive to parent-child relationships. He said in Ephesians 6:4:

> And now a word to you parents. Don't keep on scolding and nagging your children, making them angry and resentful. Rather, bring them up with the loving discipline the Lord himself approves, with suggestions and godly advice.

Discipline and love. Contradictory? No—a process that can make a young boy a wise man.

Clearly, discipline is to be handed out with a degree of discernment and lots of love: "Fathers, don't scold your children so much that they become discouraged and quit trying" (Colossians 3:21). A parent must not break a child's spirit. Instead, he must be the channel for God's Spirit to flow into the child.

A discussion about the role of parents would not be complete without a reminder of the responsibilities of children: "Moses gave you this law from God. 'Honor your father and mother.' And he said that anyone who speaks against his father or mother must die" (Mark 7:10). If these qualities are missing, Moses said, death may occur. It is not always physical death; it may be emotional or spiritual death.

> But you say it is perfectly all right for a man to disregard his needy parents, telling them, "Sorry, I can't help you! For I have given to God what I could have given

to you." And so you break the law of God in order to protect your man-made tradition. . . .

Mark 7:11—13

All parents at one time were children. The parents' role goes back to the oft-repeated Golden Rule: "Do unto others as you would have them do to you" (*see* Matthew 7:12).

For I, too, was once a son, tenderly loved by my mother as an only child, and the companion of my father. He told me never to forget his words. "If you follow them," he said, "you will have a long and happy life. *Learn to be wise,*" he said, *"and develop good judgment and common sense! I cannot overemphasize this point.*" Cling to wisdom—she will protect you. Love her—she will guard you.

Proverbs 4:3–6

Parents as well as children make mistakes. The beginning of the end to the generation gap comes when parent and child admit their errors and respond to each other in love —a very difficult task! By putting pride aside, it can be done.

Determination to be wise is the first step toward becoming wise! And with your wisdom, develop common sense and good judgment. If you exalt wisdom, she will exalt you. Hold her fast and she will lead you to great honor; she will place a beautiful crown upon your head. My son, listen to me and do as I say, and you will have a long, good life.

I would have you learn this great fact: that a life of

doing right is the wisest life there is. If you live that kind of life, you'll not limp or stumble as you run. Carry out my instructions; don't forget them, for they will lead you to real living.

Don't do as the wicked do. Avoid their haunts—turn away, go somewhere else, for evil men don't sleep until they've done their evil deed for the day. They can't rest unless they cause someone to stumble and fall. They eat and drink wickedness and violence!

But the good man walks along in the ever-brightening light of God's favor; the dawn gives way to morning splendor, while the evil man gropes and stumbles in the dark.

Listen, son of mine, to what I say. Listen carefully. Keep these thoughts ever in mind; let them penetrate deep within your heart, for they will mean real life for you, and radiant health.

Above all else, guard your affections. For they influence everything else in your life. Spurn the careless kiss of a prostitute. Stay far from her. Look straight ahead; don't even turn your head to look. Watch your step. Stick to the path and be safe. Don't sidetrack; pull back your foot from danger.

Proverbs 4:7–27

What marvelous advice! Imagine how a child—or an adult, for that matter—must feel when his father is straightforward and honest about the things of the world. There is an openness between them, a feeling of teamwork.

Isn't it worth the extra effort to build the bridge of communication so the wheels of life will roll smoothly?

The Home as a Center for Communication

The Christian home is not only a hub for meaningful experiences, it is also a center for communication.

Frequently, families get involved with the father's professional commitments, the mother's job or social affairs, and the kids' lessons and sports events. These are important aspects of family living—essential for a balanced life. But the point to remember is that unless parents set a time and create an atmosphere for communication and initiate discussion when children are young, communication may never develop properly.

Some families never discuss anything because they "never have anything to say." Others say, "Every time we start to talk about something it ends in an argument." But have you ever talked to a family that regularly sits down to share the day's activities?

There are often interruptions by those overeager to share, and tears by those who feel discriminated against. But when it becomes a regular affair, a bond of understanding develops. This is often the one family activity that can remedy a potential problem before it erupts. Listening ears and loving hearts find a way to overcome arguments, hurt feelings, and aggressiveness.

The Home as a Center for Community Action

The Christian home must move into the community or it will become ingrown. Family members dispersed throughout the community are able to provide support posts. They hold society together. Where would we be if we didn't have those faithful children at school welcoming the frightened new students, or the welcome hostess at church or parent-teacher functions? What about the volunteer workers in the hospitals and rest homes? If responsible individuals were not on planning commissions, city councils, and environmental-control boards, we would be in a disastrous situation. In fact, in some cases we are in a bad way because some Christian men and women are placidly sitting at home having fellowship only with their Christian friends.

At one time in Jesus' ministry, an expert on Jewish law wanted to test Jesus' orthodoxy. He asked:

> "Teacher, what does a man need to do to live forever in heaven?"
>
> Jesus replied, "What does Moses' law say about it?"
>
> "It says," he replied, "that you must love the Lord your God with all your heart, and with all your soul, and with all your strength, and with all your mind. And you must love your neighbor just as much as you love yourself."
>
> "Right!" Jesus told him. *"Do* this and *you* shall live!"
>
> The man wanted to justify (his lack of love for some kinds of people), so he asked, "Which neighbors?"
>
> Luke 10:25–29

Jesus told him about the Good Samaritan. A Jewish man was attacked by robbers. People who passed his way weren't interested in helping him. They didn't want to be bothered. It wasn't until a Samaritan, who was despised by Jews, cared enough to stop that the victim received aid.

The man or woman you pass on the street or sit beside at the next meeting or on the subway is your neighbor—your sister or brother. If this is a new concept for you, it will hound you for a long time. That's good. When your heart accepts the transplant of Christ's love after removal of self-love you are on your way to dynamic living.

A strong hub brings happiness as well as motivation not only for the family but for the church, the school, and the community.

Accept the challenge. Dare to discipline. Learn to love. Your family will be the example for many others searching for success.

The Home as a Center for Nurture

The home is the nurturing center for an individual. Home is the place where children should first be able to obtain their freedom under the protection of caring parents. Normally, as a child matures he obtains more and more freedom until he is physically free of the bonds of his parents. Ironically, a child moves from parental control to cultural dominance.

If the child has had an emotionally secure home and education he is usually able to cope with his culture. However, children moved from foster home to foster home, and those of unwed mothers or absent fathers, have particular needs. Our society has attempted to deal with these situations but, unfortunately, has not been very successful. For example, the need for foster homes in California—and undoubtedly in the nation—doubled in an eight-year period. And more foster homes are needed because of the disintegration of the family and the breakdown of the family group. California officials have found that foster parents provide a level of care for children that gives them a family-life experience—the love, security, and understanding they have missed.

A growing number of unwed mothers are keeping their children. They are discovering a new sense of security with greater responsibility. On the other hand, they find their freedom has been limited. Studies show that unwed mothers tend to be incapable of meeting the physical and emotional needs of their offspring. Thus, the child put into a foster home usually has severe emotional problems upon his arrival.

Forty-six percent of children in foster homes are victims of absent fathers. Of these, only one father out of forty-three contributes to his child in some way. Only one in six men contributes to the support of his children who are on welfare.

The fathers may be released from having to support their offspring, but what sort of oppression does this foist on the children? Nothing is more pathetic than to hear a man or woman discuss freedom, liberation, and oppression and know that in the process of "finding their freedom" they stunted the growth of their child.

We need to be sure of our own identity. We must be aware that fears, frustrations, and physical limitations are natural. We need to realize that not only women but also men need to deal with the same emotions—to differing degrees.

As adults we need to see that we are the pacesetters for the younger generation. Boys and girls look to us for leadership. It is important to help them face death, failure, the Space Age, and insecurity. We can be successful only after we have dealt with these issues ourselves. We must understand the home as a nurturing center. We must comprehend the role of the mother and the father as well as other relatives in our mobile society.

Barbie, Francie, and Ken, the popular dolls, have taken the spotlight away from Raggedy Ann and Andy.

A group of ten-year-old girls playing dolls with Barbie, Ken, and Francie and their many friends, soon learns there is no flow between girlhood and motherhood anymore. Many girls between the ages of ten and twelve years are fighting for freedom to grow up at their own pace, but their parents are too eager for their daughters to have everything *now*.

I am deeply concerned that baby dolls are given to children under five years of age, and that older dolls make the scene by the time their owners are age six—long before they have matured socially and intellectually. What about the few who still go from the stuffed doll to the cuddly, look-alive doll that drinks, wets, and moves its head? We need to get over the notion that dolls and playing house are sexist ideas. It is normal for little boys and girls to role-play house and for them to role-play mommies and daddies and any other family member—or animal, for that matter. The child who is allowed to grow up at a normal rate is going to accept his adult life more realistically.

I recently read about the Hare Krishna school for children. These children are placed in a monastic atmosphere from the ages of four and one-half to eleven years. The single goal of the school is to make priests of the boys. The girls are educated to be servants to their husbands. They are to remain childlike after marriage, which occurs just prior to puberty. Many of the children in this school apparently came from broken homes or from parents too strung out on drugs to care for them.

Parents need to realize that their own childhood may not have been as secure as they would have liked. But that is no reason to pressure children to grow up and attain adulthood before they are emotionally and physically ready—or to place them in an institution that will ruin the life of a child more than the lives of his parents.

A preteen girl should have all the excitement and joy of daydreaming and thinking about what she will do when she grows up and becomes a young lady—whether it means a career, motherhood, or both.

There are mothers who are eager for their daughters to start dating boys before they reach their teen years. But, take heart! Many other parents are saying, "There are so many other fine things for our daughter or son to do that we will not allow them to date until they are sixteen years old." This, of course, is not to prohibit parties at school or in the homes of friends. But so far as official dating goes, there are too many things young people can do—and can do only at their age—without us pressuring them into early matrimony.

As a teacher I have seen many young schoolgirls wearing the latest teen-fad clothing—even when they are only ten years old. Their mothers are eager for their daughters to be part of the "in" group. But I question whether or not this is the best approach. I believe in style and essentials (bras, hose, and moderate makeup) at the proper time and in the proper place. But we do not want to overemphasize the fad forces that are constantly at work in our country. I like to see myself as being *in* the world but not *of* it.

Not long ago I heard a person comment that the bubble umbrella was indicative of our society. This type of umbrella insures a person's protection from the rain but it is not designed so that it can be shared and thus keep others out of the storm.

I do not want my children to be that isolated. It is important that they learn from their peers as well as their parents. They need to observe varied life-styles. That is part of our free country and part of maintaining a democratic society.

The Home as a Center for Responsibility

Families that are capable of raising their children to respect and honor others should be admired.

A man and woman named Amram and Jochebed are among these couples. They raised their children in Old Testament times to be responsible and reverent. However, each new generation seems to rebel in some way and their children were no different from youth today.

Amram and Jochebed had a daughter whom they named Miriam. By the time Miriam was twelve or thirteen years old, she had two younger brothers, Aaron and Moses. The youngest, Moses, was born in Egypt during the time when all male children were to be killed.

Miriam, Aaron, Amram, and Jochebed dearly loved Moses and didn't want anything to happen to him. They decided Miriam should take Moses in a little reed basket and place him in the Nile River in hopes that someone would find him and he would thus be saved. Not only did a princess from the king's court find him, but she asked Miriam to find a wet nurse. Miriam ran home and got her mother. Moses received the early nurturing so important for one of God's chosen leaders—though it was kept a secret at the time that Jochebed was his mother.

As the story unfolds in the Old Testament, Moses rebelled against Egypt's ruler. Moses had compassion for his people. Miriam, honored at being the sister of the leader of the Israelites, asserted herself into a role of leadership after the group crossed the Red Sea. She gathered the women together and they began to sing and play their timbrels.

Forty years is a long time for thousands of men, women, and children to live together, and even the children of God had moments of divisiveness. Moses had married a Cushite woman named Zipporah. Miriam was disgusted that her brother had married a non-Jew. With the support of Aaron, she gossiped her disapproval.

God, displeased with Miriam's actions, struck her with leprosy, alienating her from the group for seven days. Moses pleaded with God to heal her. After a time of restoration and a purification ceremony, she rejoined her people. But she withdrew from public attention from then on and died toward the close of the Israelites' wanderings in the wilderness of Kadesh about 1400 B.C.

What does Miriam's story tell us? Since she was the oldest of three children, great responsibility was placed upon her shoulders. As she grew up and understood the plight of her people, she felt called upon to pour all of her energies into liberating those who had been oppressed. Miriam had no desire, so far as we know, to be married or to achieve a name for herself. She was part of a united effort to set her nation free.

Many women today feel they have a responsibility to make America free of crime, Communist infiltration, and business fraud. We need more Miriams. But they need to keep their eyes on the purpose to which they have been called.

9

The Proverbial ABCs

Many people ask, "Where is a woman's place?" The writer of Proverbs says, "The wisest women build up their homes" (*see* Proverbs 14:1).

But what about the woman who calls herself a radical feminist? She is "never content to stay at home. She is loud and wayward, now in the market, lying in wait at every corner" (*see* Proverbs 7:11, 12).

Don't be shocked, Christian sister, if you meet a feminist standing next to you at the check-out counter at the market. Take a few moments to look at her. Smile. Be friendly. See her as your sister—a child of your Father whom you want to have as your friend. She has fears, frustrations, and feelings just like you. Remember when you wished for a sincere friend?

The Book of Proverbs in the Old Testament is a collection of acrostic poems which many of us either take for granted or (more likely) feel are beyond our understanding. Frequently I turn to a proverb when I need a bit of instruction and I soon discover it has something vital. It is not difficult reading. In fact, the Proverbs as contained in the Living Bible are a delightful means of learning.

I am often drawn to one particular proverb which tells about good women and unworthy wives. There are several proverbs on that subject. And there are some good proverbs for men, too!

My favorite proverb is the thirty-first, the last one in the book (see Proverbs 31:10–31). This chapter is referred to by some scholars as the Proverbial ABCs of womanhood. This passage was undoubtedly written by a Jew in the postexilic period, or perhaps earlier. Tradition has assigned the authorship to King Lemuel.

I have discovered the teachings in the Proverbs refer to women with high standards of chastity and marital fidelity. Monogamous relationships, great respect for all women, and condemnation of those who disobey the law are cardinal points.

A good wife is respected, admired, and loved. The life she leads shows her to be a worthy woman.

The godly woman to whom Lemuel refers is a "professional" woman with a full-time job. Her life centers around many economic activities. She provides clothing (she has a God-given major in home economics), does the buying and selling (a God-given major in retailing), takes an active role in business, and displays prudence and wise management in all matters (a God-given major in public relations).

The modern woman finds herself in a community-leadership role. She becomes aware of her role as a teacher and counselor. As a mother she is available to answer her children's questions and handle their unstable emotions as well as to share their joys. As a community leader she is helping to set an atmosphere and motivate other women.

Today's woman must be a godly woman if she is to succeed in her diversified roles.

Proverbs 31:10–31 could be called the Proverbial ABCs because of the way it was written in the Hebrew. The first letter of each verse follows the order of the Hebrew alphabet. Crawford H. Toy calls this chapter the "golden ABC of the perfect wife."

Anyone who reads this proverb will admit it is difficult to find a woman with such qualities. It claims a good wife is a man's treasure—she is worth more than jewels. What a contradiction when you read in the newspapers that a husband gave his wife a jewel valued at several million dollars and then several years later he separates from her. This is not a marriage, it is a mirage. Any man who attempts to crown his wife by his own doing is in for grief. The only way a wife can become a man's jewel is for him to first belong to God.

> If you can find a truly good wife, she is worth more than precious gems! Her husband can trust her, and she will richly satisfy his needs. She will not hinder him, but help him all her life. She finds wool and flax and busily spins it. She buys imported foods, brought by ship from distant ports. She gets up before dawn to prepare breakfast for her household, and plans the day's work for her servant girls. She goes out to inspect a field, and buys it; with her own hands she plants a vineyard. She is energetic, a hard worker, and watches for bargains. She works far into the night!
>
> She sews for the poor, and generously gives to the needy. She has no fear of winter for her household, for she has made warm clothes for all of them. She also upholsters with finest tapestry; her own clothing is beautifully made—a purple gown of pure linen. Her husband is well known, for he sits in the council chamber with the other civic leaders. She makes belted linen garments to sell to the merchants.

107

She is a woman of strength and dignity, and has no fear of old age. When she speaks, her words are wise, and kindness is the rule for everything she says. She watches carefully all that goes on throughout her household, and is never lazy. Her children stand and bless her; so does her husband. He praises her with these words:

"There are many fine women in the world, but you are the best of them all!"

Charm can be deceptive and beauty doesn't last, but a woman who fears and reverences God shall be greatly praised. Praise her for the many fine things she does. These good deeds of hers shall bring her honor and recognition from even the leaders of the nations.

Proverbs 31:10–31

A godly woman is strong and virtuous. She has great worth because, like a rare jewel, she is hard to find.

It is mandatory for parents not only to instruct a daughter about her place in the world but also to teach a son that he may have to look a long time before he finds the right woman. "The man who finds a wife finds a good thing; she is a blessing to him from the Lord" (Proverbs 18:22).

A man's heart must trust his wife. The Hebrew meaning for the word "heart" is "mind." This makes it more difficult since our hearts are often governed by emotion. Our minds must be made to see the whole person.

Not only are a husband's affections involved but his confidence in his wife's ability to manage a home and to be faithful is also important. She must be strong enough to care for the physical, aesthetic, and emotional climate of the home.

The author of the Book of Proverbs advises a man who desires a good companion and a godly woman, "Let her charms and, tender embrace satisfy you. Let her love alone fill you with delight" (5:19). When a man has this type of woman he lacks nothing. He has his wealth; he needs nothing more to succeed.

A major question has arisen regarding the institution of marriage: Is it bad? It is written in Proverbs 21:9 that it is better to live alone in an attic than share a palace with a nagging wife.

A husband has a major responsibility to recognize the uniqueness of his wife. If a man finds a woman who is loyal, good, and loving, Her worth is far beyond jewels (see Proverbs 31:10). If he reveres her, he will find that her delight is making him happy. The work she does with her hands will be done willingly and with great joy.

I especially like the verse, "She gets up before dawn to prepare breakfast for her household . . ." (Proverbs 31:15). How many women are up early preparing the most important meal of the day for their families? Many take advantage of the instant hot cereals and all of those candy-coated cold creations, not to mention the instant liquid-breakfasts and breakfast bars.

After teaching a nutrition course to a group of young people in the 4-H Club, I realized how little they knew about the subject. Nutritionists are discovering that processed foods lack major nutrients even though the package says the product is fortified with vitamins.

A little earlier to bed will make the morning alarm sound a little less harsh when it calls you to get up and feed your husband and family. A little more sleep will also allow you to start the day in a better mood.

Recently I was attacked by a viral bug that made me very

weak. I started dreading the morning alarm from the moment I went to bed the night before. Some mornings I was physically unable to get up but when I regained some of my strength and made the all-American effort (for some, it's vanishing, too), I received great satisfaction seeing my children going off to school after a nutritious breakfast, carrying lunch pails containing a balanced noon meal.

How many women have some form of a vegetable garden in the spring, summer, and fall? If it is nothing more than an herb garden on the windowsill, it is a way of providing a natural richness for your cookery. This past spring and summer I noticed that a number of magazines carried stories about gardens for small locations. One squash plant can become a ground cover and save you several dollars. No matter where you live, or how little space you have, work out a plan to provide some fresh vegetables for your family this next year.

During the postexilic period women had to obtain their fabrics from far-off lands. Today there are sewing centers relatively near every home. Even with the rising prices of fabrics, a woman can make a pantsuit, caftan, or some lingerie for half of the retail price.

For the last several years my family and I have been active in the 4-H program. One of the most rewarding of the various events is the Dress Revue. The creativity is amazing; the garments are made for a fraction of their cost in the store.

There is a big flap over how women spend their time. Some say they spend too much time in the car running errands. Proverbs 31:14 claims, ". . . like the ships of the merchant, she brings her food from afar" (RSV). Could we think of our pickups, cars, and station wagons as our "ships"?

A godly woman uses time wisely. An all-morning coffee klatch is an invitation to gossip. But a dialogue with another woman about responsibilities and rewards in and outside of the home can be profitable to both people. Because the godly woman is sensitive to her husband, he has the opportunity to use his talents. He is able to mingle with key businessmen and colleagues in his line of work.

The godly woman is proud not only of what she is able to do for her family and society, but also of her gracefulness in growing older. To have a high-school or college diploma is always good insurance, but a person's capabilities come from experience gained through the years.

The Proverbs writer says, "She is clothed in dignity and power, and can afford to laugh at tomorrow" (see Proverbs 31:25 RSV).

When my child says, "You're the best, Mommy," I realize how far short I fall of being God's perfect woman. But that doesn't matter. All He cares about is my relationship to Him: my attitude and willingness to yield—first to God, then to my husband and children.

Outer beauty may fade with the years, but the beauty inside will be a glow forever!

10

The Crown of Jewels

My life will continually be changing, but in many ways, the major hurdles of liberation have been jumped. My greatest desire is to be a godly woman. Although I can never measure up to all the requirements, I can seek "God's greatest for God's gal" (the motto for Seek Out—a program of seminars for women led by the author).

I count it a privilege to be liberated through Christ's love. And now I humbly seek the crown of jewels.

Don't be concerned about the outward beauty that depends on jewelry, or beautiful clothes, or hair arrangement. Be beautiful inside, in your hearts, with the lasting charm of a gentle and quiet spirit which is so precious to God. That kind of deep beauty was seen in the saintly women of old, who trusted God and fitted in with their husbands' plans.
1 Peter 3:3–5

The crown of jewels consists of God's richest fruits: love, joy, peace, patience, kindness, goodness, faithfulness, gentleness, and self-control. These are not forbidden fruits. They belong to us when our lives are submitted to Jesus Christ.

There is no way you can earn these jewels. They are given as a lifetime investment. Just as you can lose a jewel from a ring or bracelet if it is not periodically checked by a jeweler, so you also can lose the jewels in your crown if you take your life away from Jesus.

Our birthright is being a woman. Our birth certificates state names given to us by our parents but our lives as liberated women can only begin when we say:

Dear God, I am a sinner. I need You. I may not know You very well but You know me and I desire to be made known to others by Your fruits within me. At this moment, I relinquish my entire being—everything. Help me as I seek the power of Your Holy Spirit in my life for Jesus' sake. Amen.

If we have sincerely uttered this prayer, God will present us with the basic crown of life. He will set the jewels in our crown as we grow in His Spirit. Our responsibility is to prepare our hearts each day through prayer and reading the Scriptures; to seek His will. We will not only *be* liberated —we will *feel* it!

The theme Bible verse for liberation is First Corinthians 11:11, 12: "(Nevertheless, in the Lord woman is not independent of man nor man of woman; for as woman was made from man, so man is now born of woman. And all things are from God)" (RSV).

It is not a matter of the "haves" and the "have nots." It is the maturity a person has to recognize the divine plan for the two sexes.

Shortly after the parade along the Santa Cruz Mall during the Ms. California Counter Pageant, I interviewed a man on the street who quoted a well-known homily:

"God did not take woman from man's head that he might Lord it over her; or from his feet that he might tread on her; or from his arms to abuse her, but he took Eve from Adam's side—closest to his heart that he might love, revere, and cherish her."

In this, God dignified womanhood. In so-called Christian nations, womanhood has been respected. I am sad that womankind today has so little personal regard for the place God gave her as a helpmeet, mother, and homemaker that she now attempts to frustrate this privilege and position by emulating man and, in a sense, abdicating her God-given prerogatives.

Man should live by the sweat of his brow. If womankind now chooses a place where she wants to change sweetness for sweat, I presume she has the right to make her choice. In my mind, she demeans and removes herself from the pedestal of perfection and respect that I personally choose to regard as womankind's place in the world.

Another man, referring to the parade, said, "These women show a total rebellion against God."

Others were less harsh. One man remarked, "Oh, let them have their fun. Maybe it will help them get rid of their frustrations."

It is obvious that feminists do not have peace. They are caught up in a world that will continually oppress them because they do not allow themselves to be liberated by the Liberator.

A decision about your life must be made. Let me guide you, dear sister. Take a few moments. Think about what you have read.

The crown of jewels is offered to you. But wait. There are

three requirements you must meet before the gift is yours. First, you must have a purpose:

> I press on toward the goal for the prize of the upward call of God in Christ Jesus. Let those of us who are mature be thus minded; and if in anything you are otherwise minded, God will reveal that also to you. Only let us hold true to what we have attained.
>
> Philippians 3:14–16 RSV

It is a high and holy calling to belong to the King and to exalt Him. It is good to be part of that sisterhood.

The second requirement is to praise the Creator. You will find the command to praise throughout the Bible: "Let everything that breathes praise the LORD! Praise the LORD!" (Psalms 150:6 RSV). "Praise the Lord, all Gentiles, and let all the peoples praise him" (Romans 15:11 RSV). "For it is written, 'As I live, says the Lord, every knee shall bow to me, and every tongue shall give praise to God' " (Romans 14:11 RSV). "My mouth is filled with thy praise, and with thy glory all the day" (Psalms 71:8 RSV).

Prayer is the third requirement for the crown of jewels. Before praying, look at the Scriptures. What does Jesus say about prayer? His most famous discourse is Matthew 7:7, 8 RSV: "Ask, and it will be given you; seek, and you will find; knock, and it will be opened to you. For every one who asks receives, and he who seeks finds, and to him who knocks it will be opened."

> But when you pray, go into your room and shut the door and pray to your Father who is in secret; and your

Father who sees in secret will reward you. . . . For if you forgive men their trespasses, your heavenly Father also will forgive you; but if you do not forgive men their trespasses, neither will your Father forgive your trespasses.

Matthew 6:6,14,15 RSV

Live prayer. Many times we receive instructions to set aside a prayer time. This is an excellent idea, but it is inadequate. Plan a definite time of prayer, preferably first thing in the morning when your body is rested and your mind is unencumbered with the thoughts of the day.

More important, make prayer an ongoing conversation with God. "Continue steadfastly in prayer, being watchful in it with thanksgiving" (Colossians 4:2 RSV). When the Holy Spirit brings an individual or instance to mind, that is when you are commissioned to pray. It takes a deep prayer commitment to make yourself available to God's Spirit and the needs of your fellow man all of the time.

God is not only the Master Planner; He is also the Master Engineer. We must not schedule our time so tightly that He is unable to use us.

Not long ago I read a column by Abigail Van Buren that told of Mr. O.L. Crain, a member of the Typographical Union, local number 283 in Oklahoma City. He wrote a poem as a "gentle reminder that employees who work at a steady pace without hurrying do better work and more of it than those who need a slowing down!"

The prayer has been passed around and even changed. But he sent the original, which has never been copyrighted, to Abigail and wrote, "I am well paid if it makes you happy.

117

Keep it or share it with your friends."

Slow me down, Lord!
Ease the pounding of my heart
By the quieting of my mind.
Steady my hurried pace
With a vision of the eternal reach
    of time.

Give me,
Amidst the confusion of my day,
The calmness of the everlasting hills.
Break the tensions of my nerves
With the soothing music of the
    singing streams
That live in my memory.

Help me to know
The magical restoring power of sleep.
Teach me the art
Of taking minute vacations of
    slowing down
    to look at a flower;
    to chat with an old friend or
        make a new one;
    to pat a stray dog;
    to watch a spider build a web;
    to smile at a child;
    or to read a few lines from a good
        book.

Remind me each day
That the race is not always to the
    swift;

That there is more to life than
increasing its speed.

Let me look upward
Into the branches of the towering oak,
And know that it grew great and strong
Because it grew slowly and well.

Slow me down, Lord,
And inspire me to send my roots deep
Into the soil of life's enduring values
That I may grow toward the stars
Of my greater destiny.

Listen to what God has to say. Sometimes we are so busy
complaining or confessing that God can't communicate
with us. "Rest in the Lord; wait patiently for him to act
. . ." (Psalms 37:7). "Stand silent! Know that I am God! I will
be honored by every nation in the world!" (Psalms 46:10).
When enjoying fellowship with God, allow your body to
relax. Let His Spirit refresh your soul.

When we have a purpose, praise the Lord, and practice
prayer, we are ready to have jewels placed in our crown.
Some of the first jewels recognized will be the fruits received from God's Spirit: "But when the Holy Spirit controls
our lives he will produce this kind of fruit in us: love, joy,
peace, patience, kindness, goodness, faithfulness, gentleness and self-control . . ." (Galatians 5:22,23). These fruits
are evident in the Spirit-filled life.

If our lives do not bear fruit, we become useless to God:
"The axe of his judgment is poised over you, ready to sever
your roots and cut you down. Yes, every tree that does not
produce good fruit will be chopped down and thrown into

the fire" (Luke 3:9). In order to become recognized or known, our fruits must be visible. This is what catches the eye of the person struggling for peace with God.

The results of being faithful are not only fruits but also a freedom for living not known to our feminist sisters:

> Heaven can be entered only through the narrow gate! The highway to hell is broad, and its gate is wide enough for all the multitudes who choose its easy way. But the Gateway to Life is small, and the road is narrow, and only a few ever find it.
>
> Matthew 7:13,14

It is wonderful to know that we have the freedom to choose the gate by which we will enter eternity. What part of the Feminist Movement can offer this option?

We have the choice of eternal life and we may also choose how we will live now. Jesus said:

> Don't worry about whether you have enough food to eat or clothes to wear. For life consists of far more than food and clothes. Look at the ravens—they don't plant or harvest or have barns to store away their food, and yet they get along all right—for God feeds them. And you are far more valuable to him than any birds!
>
> And besides, what's the use of worrying? What good does it do? Will it add a single day to your life? Of course not! And if worry can't even do such little things as that, what's the use of worrying over bigger things?
>
> Luke 12:22–26

Remember, the free gift of God is eternal life. The Apostle Paul reminds us ''. . . the wages of sin is death, but the free gift of God is eternal life through Jesus Christ our Lord'' (Romans 6:23). This is a gift. It cannot be bought or bargained for. It is impossible to earn. We are but visitors on this earth: ''Since your real home is in heaven I beg you to keep away from the evil pleasures of this world; they are not for you, for they fight against your very souls'' (1 Peter 2:11).

But don't forget this, dear friends, that a day or a thousand years from now is like tomorrow to the Lord. He isn't really being slow about his promised return, even though it sometimes seems that way. But he is waiting, for the good reason that he is not willing that any should perish, and he is giving more time for sinners to repent. The day of the Lord is surely coming, as unexpectedly as a thief, and then the heavens will pass away with a terrible noise and the heavenly bodies will disappear in fire, and the earth and everything on it will be burned up.

2 Peter 3:8–10

Last, by being faithful we receive far more than we could ever give. We receive the gift of eternal life. And we receive gifts to be used in this earthly existence. Each individual has different gifts. You have something unique to contribute to society.

Some spiritual gifts are prophecy, teaching, healing, speaking in unknown languages, and being an apostle or prophet. But the greatest gift is love. This gift is essential in order to live the abundant life. It is the most important gift of all. In its purest form, it is God.

Liberation? Liberation from what?

From feelings of inferiority; from self-imposed pressures of "I have to do this. . . ." "I have to join that. . . ." "I have to . . . I must . . . I should. . . ."

We are career women, homemakers, or whatever by profession; we are liberated by choice.

Remember that at the next Women's Liberation demonstration. The people you see are searching for the self-confidence and freedom that others—maybe you—have already found.

As good citizens, we need to improve working conditions and provide equal pay for women. But let's not surrender the beautiful rights of our God-given, biological sex. God made us female for a purpose—let's be joyous about it! Let's enjoy the liberation that is our personal gift.

Open that gift. Allow Jesus Christ, by the power of His Spirit, to guide you and make you lovingly liberated!